Essays on
THE DEATH PENALTY

EDITED BY

T. ROBERT INGRAM

i

LIBRARY OF CONGRESS CATALOGUE

CARD NO. 63-21970

FIRST PRINTING 1963

SECOND PRINTING 1971

ST. THOMAS PRESS
P. O. BOX 35096
HOUSTON, TEXAS 77035

PRINTED IN U.S.A.

Table of Contents

Introduction

Presented here in one volume are the writings of several Christian men about the Christian system of law and order as it rests upon the execution of the death penalty after "due process" as the chief punishment for crime against God. Most of the writers are ordained ministers in one of the recognized Christian denominations, but not all. C. S. Lewis has achieved personal rank as a spokesman for Christ wherever English is the common tongue, although he is not of the cloth. He is Fellow of Magdalene College and Professor of Medieval and Renaissance English at the University of Cambridge and known throughout the world as author of the delightful "Screwtape Letters" and other popular treatments of Christian doctrine.

Gervas A. Carey is a Quaker, formerly President of George Fox College in Oregon, Pastor and Professor of Bible, now living in Honolulu. G. Aiken Taylor is a strong leader in the so-called Southern Presbyterian Church, an ordained minister and editor of THE PRESBYTERIAN JOURNAL. W. A. Barnett is Deacon of the Baptist Church of Moncks Corner, South Carolina.

E. L. H. Taylor, a priest of the Church of England, had a vigorous parish ministry in Canada for several years, then returned to England to continue parish work there. He is author of a number of works on public affairs. Jacob J. Vellenga represents another denominational allegiance, having served since 1958 as Associate Executive of the

United Presbyterian Church in the U.S.A. T. Robert Ingram is a priest of the Protestant Episcopal Church of the United States, Rector of St. Thomas' Church and School, Houston, Texas.

In anticipation of the question, "Do these men speak for their denominations?", it should be remarked that no Christian minister professes to speak for "the Church" or any Church. He speaks for Jesus Christ, being a minister of the Gospel of Christ, called of God. The Church does not set policy or ordain truth: She merely bears witness to the Word of God and the Faith once delivered into the charge of the people of God. The test of true proclamation of the Word is whether it is in accord with Scripture interpreted by the faith that the Christ spoken of by the Prophets has come in the flesh of Jesus and that He, crucified and risen from the dead, is now sovereign Lord over all things, including governments and law and order.

None of the writings here was prepared for this volume. All except E. L. H. Taylor's second piece on "Medicine or Morals, etc." have appeared in print elsewhere, and some have been reprinted in several publications. While the studies have been made independently by men who, for the most part, have never even met each other, their remarkable singleness of thought can be explained by the fact that Christian doctrine does not change. Faith in Christ is truly catholic in the usual sense of that word as being of "all men, everywhere, always." True declaration of the Faith is not a matter of opinion, but an inescapable line of reason and experience that must follow upon the confession that Jesus is Lord.

THE EDITOR

The Humanitarian Theory
of Punishment

by

C. S. LEWIS

In England we have lately had a controversy about capital punishment. I do not know whether a murderer is more likely to repent and make a good end on the gallows a few weeks after his trial or in the prison infirmary thirty years later. I do not know whether the fear of death is an indispensable deterrent. I need not, for the purpose of this article, decide whether it is a morally permissible deterrent. Those are questions which I propose to leave untouched. My subject is not capital punishment in particular, but that theory of punishment in general which the controversy showed to be almost universal among my fellow countrymen. It may be called the humanitarian theory. Those who hold it think that it is mild and merciful. In this I believe that they are seriously mistaken. I believe that the "humanity" which it claims is a dangerous illusion and disguises the possibility of cruelty and injustice without end. I urge a return to the traditional or retributive theory not solely, not even primarily, in the interests of society, but in the interests of the criminal.

— According to the humanitarian theory, to punish a man because he deserves it, and as much as he deserves, is mere revenge, and, therefore, barbarous and immoral. It is maintained that the only legitimate motives for punishing are the desire to deter others by example or to mend the criminal. When this theory is combined, as frequently happens, with the belief that all crime is more or less pathological, the idea of mending tails off into that of healing. Punishment becomes therapeutic.

Thus it appears at first sight that we have passed from the harsh and self-righteous notion of giving the wicked their deserts to the charitable and enlightened one of tending the psychologically sick. What could be more amiable? One little point which is taken for granted in this theory needs, however, to be made explicit. The things done to the criminal, even if they are called cures, will be just as compulsory as they were in the old days when we called them punishments. If a tendency to steal can be cured by psychotherapy, the thief will no doubt be forced to undergo treatment. Otherwise, society cannot continue.

My contention is that this doctrine, merciful though it appears, really means that each one of us, from the moment he breaks the law, is deprived of the rights of a human being.

The reason is this. The humanitarian theory removes from punishment the concept of desert. But the concept of desert is the only connecting link between punishment and justice. It is only as deserved or undeserved that a sentence can be just or unjust. I do not here contend that the question "Is it deserved?" is the only one we can reasonably ask about a punishment. We may very properly ask whether it is likely to deter others and to reform the criminal.

But neither of these two last questions is a question about justice. There is no sense in talking about a "just deterrent" or a "just cure." We demand of a deterrent not whether it is just but whether it succeeds. Thus when we cease to consider what will cure him or deter others, we have tacitly removed him from the sphere of justice altogether; instead of a person, a subject of rights, we now have a mere object, a patient, a "case" to be treated in a clinic.

The distinction will become clearer if we ask who will be qualified to determine sentences when sentences are no longer held to derive their propriety from the criminal's deservings. In the old view, the problem of fixing the right sentence was a moral problem. Accordingly, the judge who did it was a person trained in jurisprudence; trained, that is, in a science which deals with rights and duties, and which, in origin at least, was consciously accepting guidance from the law of nature, and from Scripture. We must admit that in the actual penal code of most countries at most times these high originals were so much modified by local custom, class interests, and utilitarian concessions, as to be very imperfectly recognizable. But the code was never in principle, and not always in fact, beyond the control of the conscience of society. And when (say, in eighteenth century England) actual punishments conflicted too violently with the moral sense of the community, juries refused to convict, and reform was finally brought about.

This was possible because, so long as we are thinking in terms of desert, the propriety of the penal code, being a moral question, is a question on which every man has the right to an opinion, not because he follows this or that profession, but because he is simply a man, rational animal enjoying the natural light. But all this is changed when we drop the concept of desert. The only two questions we may now ask about a punishment are whether it deters and whether it cures.

But these are not questions on which anyone is entitled to have an opinion simply because he is a man. He is not entitled to an opinion even if, in addition to being a man, he should happen also to be a jurist, a Christian, and a moral theologian. For they are not questions about principle but about matter of fact; and for such, *cuiquam in sua arte credendum* (to each his last). Only the expert "penologist" (let barbarous things have barbarous names), in the light of previous experiment, can tell us what is likely to deter; only the psychotherapist can tell us what is likely to cure. It will be in vain for the rest of us, speaking simply as men, to say, "But this punishment is hideously unjust, hideously disproportionate to the criminal's deserts." The experts with perfect logic will reply: "But nobody was talking about deserts. No one was talking about *punishment* in your archaic, vindictive sense of the word. Here are the statistics proving that this treatment deters. Here are the statistics proving that this other treatment cures. What is your trouble?"

The humanitarian theory, then, removes sentences from the hands of jurists whom the public conscience is entitled to criticize, and places them in the hands of technical experts whose special sciences do not even employ such categories as rights or justice. It might be argued that since this transference results from an abandonment of the old idea of punishment, and therefore, of all vindictive motives, it will be safe to leave our criminals in such hands. I will not pause to comment on the simple-minded view of fallen human nature which such a belief implies. Let us rather remember that the "cure" of criminals is to be compulsory; and let us then watch how the theory actually works in the mind of the humanitarian.

The immediate starting point of this article was a letter I read in one of our leftist weeklies. The author was pleading that a certain sin, now treated by our laws as a crime, should henceforward be treated as a disease. And he complained that under the present system the offender, after a term in jail, was simply let out to return to his original environment, where he would probably relapse. What he complained of was not the shutting up but the letting out. On his remedial view of punishment the offender should, of course, be detained until he was cured. And of course the official straighteners are the only people who can say when that is. The first result of the humanitarian theory is, therefore, to substitute for a definite sentence (reflecting to some extent the community's moral judgment on the degree of ill-desert involved) an indefinite sentence terminable only by the word of those experts—and they are not experts in moral theology nor even in the law of nature—who inflict it. Which of us, if he stood in the dock, would not prefer to be tried by the old system?

It may be said that by the continued use of the word punishment and the use of the verb "inflict" I am misrepresenting humanitarians. They are not punishing, not inflicting, only healing. But do not let us be deceived by a name. To be taken without consent from my home and friends; to lose my liberty; to undergo all those assaults on my personality which modern psychotherapy knows how to deliver; to be re-made after some pattern of "normality" hatched in a Viennese laboratory to which I never professed allegiance; to know that this process will never end until either my captors have succeeded or I grow wise enough to cheat them with apparent success—who cares whether this is called punishment or not? That it includes most of the elements for which any punishment is feared—shame, exile, bondage, and years eaten by the locust—is obvious. Only enormous ill-desert could justify it; but ill-desert is the very conception which the humanitarian theory has thrown overboard.

If we turn from the curative to the deterrent justification of punishment we shall find the new theory even more alarming. When you punish a man to make of him an "example" to others, you are admittedly using him as a means to an end; someone else's end. This, in itself, would be a very wicked thing to do. On the classical theory of punishment it was of course justified on the ground that the man deserved it. That was assumed to be established before any question of "making him an example" arose. You then, as the saying is, killed two birds with one stone; in the process of giving him what he deserved you set an example to others. But take away desert and the whole morality of the punishment disappears. Why, in heaven's name, am I to be sacrificed to the good of society in this way—unless, of course, I deserve it?

But that is not the worst. If the justification of exemplary punishment is not to be based on desert but solely on its efficacy as a deterrent, it is not absolutely necessary that the man we punish should even have committed the crime. The deterrent effect demands that the public should draw the moral: "If we do such an act we shall suffer like that man." The punishment of a man actually guilty whom the public think innocent will not have the desired effect; the punishment of a man actually innocent will, provided the public think him guilty. But every modern state has powers which make it easy to fake a trial. When a victim is urgently needed for exemplary purposes and a guilty victim cannot be found, all the purposes of deterrence will be equally served by the punishment (call it "cure" if you prefer) of an innocent victim, provided that the public can be cheated into thinking him guilty.

It is no use to ask me why I assume that our rulers will be so wicked. The punishment of an innocent, that is, an underserving, man is wicked only if we grant the traditional view that righteous punishment means deserved punishment. Once we have abandoned that criterion, all punishments have to be justified, if at all, on other grounds that have nothing to do with desert. Where the punishment of the innocent can be justified on those grounds (and it could in some cases be justified as a deterrent) it will be no less moral than any other punishment. Any distaste for it on the part of a humanitarian will be merely a hang-over from the retributive theory.

It is, indeed, important to notice that my argument so far supposes no evil intentions on the part of the humanitarian and considers only what is involved in the logic of his position. My contention is that good men (not bad men) consistently acting upon that position would act as cruelly and unjustly as the greatest tyrants. They might in some respects act even worse. Of all tyrannies a tyranny sincerely exercised for the good of its victims may be the most oppressive. It may be better to live under robber barons than under omnipotent moral busybodies. The robber baron's cruelty may sometimes sleep, his cupidity may at some point be satiated; but those who torment us for our own good will torment us without end, for they do so with the approval of their own conscience. They may be more likely to go to heaven yet at the same time likelier to make a hell of earth. Their very kindness stings with intolerable insult. To be "cured" against one's will and cured of states which we may not regard as disease is to be put on a level with those who have not yet reached the age of reason or those who never will; to be classed with infants, imbeciles, and domestic animals. But to be punished, however severely, because we have deserved it, because we "ought to have known better," is to be treated as a human person made in God's image.

In reality, however, we must face the possibility of bad rulers armed with a humanitarian theory of punishment. A great many popular blue prints for a Christian society are merely what the Elizabethans called "eggs in moonshine" because they assume that the whole society is Christian or that the Christians are in control. This is not so in most contemporary states. Even if it were, our rulers would still be fallen men, and, therefore, neither very wise nor very good. As it is, they will usually be unbelievers. And since wisdom and virtue are not the only nor the commonest qualifications for a place in the government, they will not often be even the best unbelievers.

The practical problem of Christian politics is not that of drawing up schemes for a Christian society, but that of living as innocently as we can with unbelieving fellow-subjects under unbelieving rulers who will never be perfectly wise and good and who will sometimes be very wicked and very foolish. And when they are wicked the humanitarian theory of punishment will put in their hands a finer instru--ment of tyranny than wickedness ever had before.

For if crime and disease are to be regarded as the same thing, it follows that any state of mind which our masters choose to call "disease" can be treated as crime; and compulsorily cured. It will be vain to plead that states of mind which displease government need not always involve moral turpitude and do not therefore always deserve forfeiture of liberty. For our masters will not be using the concepts of desert and punishment but those of disease and cure.

We know that one school of psychology already regards religion as a neurosis. When this particular neurosis becomes inconvenient to government, what is to hinder government from proceeding to "cure" it? Such "cure" will, of course, be compulsory; but under the humanitarian theory it will not be called by the shocking name of persecution. No one will blame us for being Christian, no one will hate us, no one will revile us. The new Nero will approach us with the silky manners of a doctor, and though all will be in fact as compulsory as the *tunica molesta* or Smithfield or Tyburn, all will go on within the unemotional therapeutic sphere where words like "right" and "wrong" or "freedom" and "slavery" are never heard.

And thus when the command is given, every prominent Christian in the land may vanish overnight into Institutions for the Treatment of the Ideologically Unsound, and it will rest with the expert jailers to say when (if ever) they are to re-emerge. But it will not be persecution. Even if the treatment is painful, even if it is lifelong, even if it is fatal, that will be only a regrettable accident; the intention was purely therapeutic. Even as in ordinary medicine there were painful operations and fatal operations, so in this. But because they are "treatment," not punishment, they can be criticized only by fellow experts and on technical grounds, never by men as men and on grounds of justice.

That is why I think it essential to oppose the humanitarian theory of punishment, root and branch, wherever we encounter it. It carries on its front a semblance of mercy which is wholly false. That is how it can deceive men of good will. The error began, perhaps, with Shelley's statement that the distinction between mercy and justice was invented in the courts of tyrants. It sounds noble, and was indeed the error of a noble mind. But the distinction is essential. The older view was that mercy "tempered" justice, or (on the highest level of all) that mercy and justice had met and kissed. The essential act of mercy was to pardon; and pardon in its very essence involves the recognition of guilt and ill-desert in the recipient. If crime is only a disease which needs cure, it cannot be pardoned. How can you pardon a man for having a gumboil or a club foot?

But the humanitarian theory wants simply to abolish justice and substitute mercy for it. This means you start being "kind" to people before you have considered their rights, and then force upon them supposed kindnesses which they in fact had a right to refuse, and finally kindnesses which no one but you will recognize as kindnesses and which the recipient will feel as abominable cruelties. You have overshot the mark. Mercy detached from justice grows unmerciful.

That is the important paradox. As there are plants which will flourish only in mountain soil, so it appears that mercy will flower only when it grows in the crannies of the rock of justice. Transplanted to the marshlands of mere humanitarianism, it becomes a man-eating weed, all the more dangerous because it is still called by the same name as the mountain variety. But we ought long ago to have learned our lesson. We should be too old now to be deceived by those humane pretensions which have served to usher in every cruelty of the revolutionary period in which we live. These are the "precious balms" which will "break our heads."

There is a fine sentence in Bunyan: "It came burning hot into my mind, whatever he said, and however he flattered, when he got me home to his house, he would sell me for a slave." There is a fine couplet, too, in John Ball:

Be ware ere ye be woe;
Know your friend from your foe.

II

The Death Penalty

by

E. L. H. Taylor

As the abolition of the death penalty in Canada will involve nothing less than a fundamental revolution in the present structure and conception of Canadian Law and Justice, it behooves every thinking citizen of our land to examine with the greatest care the arguments for and against abolition. Will the supposed advantages to be gained from abolition offset the legal, political and moral dangers involved in changing the whole basis upon which our penal system has up till now been operated? Is the movement for abolition merely part of a wider campaign to place the criminal law of this realm upon a purely "scientistic" basis, substituting medicine for morals as the yardstick of our criminal code? Is the new category of "psychopath" now being used by penologists to describe murderers the thin end of what will one day prove to be an enormously thick wedge, so thick that it will in fact split wide open the fundamental principles upon which our whole legal and political system is now based—undermining the principle of the responsibility of every sane adult Canadian for his own actions, his freedom to choose between good and evil and his liability to be pun-

13

ished should he prefer evil? In his classic work, "LAW OF THE CONSTITUTION," A. V. Dicey refers to the legal doctrine of individual responsibility as one of the two principles which underlie the whole law of the Constitution, and the maintenance of which has gone a great way both to ensure the supremacy of the Rule of Law and ultimately to curb the arbitrariness of the Executive branch of British states. Thus he says—

The first of these . . . is that every wrongdoer is individually responsible for every unlawful or wrongful act in which he takes a part . . . This doctrine of individual responsibility is the real foundation of the legal dogma that the orders of the King himself are no justification for the commission of a wrongful or illegal act. The ordinary rule, therefore, that every wrongdoer is individually liable for the wrong he has committed is the foundation on which rests the great constitutional doctrine of ministerial responsibility.[1]

It has been argued by Gerald Gardiner, Q.C., in his book CAPITAL PUNISHMENT AS A DETERRENT, as well as by Arthur Koestler and Lord Gowers, that the death penalty is NOT an effective and necessary deterrent, and that it should therefore be abolished.[2] The chief deterrent to criminal homicide, they suggest, is not barbarity of punishment, but certainty of conviction. According to Mr. Gardiner the experience of countries which have abolished the death penalty shows abolition has not been followed by a rise in the murder rate. Unfortunately for Mr. Gardiner's thesis the murder rates for Norway and Sweden refute his argument. If the statistics of Norway are taken in conjunction with the possibly more reliable records for Sweden they show that the murder rate is HIGHER for these two countries than for Great Britain. In fact the rate is nearly double for Norway and more than double for Sweden for the 30 years from 1910 to 1939. According to figures presented before the Royal Commission on Capital Punishment the mean rate of murders per ONE MILLION of population for the successive periods of ten years 1900-1909 etc. are: 2.54, 2.73, 2.60 for England and Wales; 5.4, 4.9, 5.0 for Norway, and 7.1, 5.0, 5.0 for Sweden. If babies are included the comparable figures become: for England, 4.1, 3.9, 3.3, and for Sweden, 12.8, 9.0, and 8.2. The death penalty was rare in Sweden after 1865, it was definitely in abeyance after 1910 and was formally abolished in 1921; in Norway it was abolished in 1905 after being thirty years in abeyance. These facts do, at least, suggest that an operative death penalty is a factor in the establishment of a lower murder rate. If England and Wales had had the same murder rates as Norway there would have been 2,800 MORE murders in the 30 years; if the same rates as Sweden, 3,500 more. In the opinion of the Royal Commission on Capital Punishment there is some evidence, though no conclusive evidence of a statistical nature, that the death penalty is likely to have a stronger deterrent effect than imprisonment on NORMAL human beings and it thinks that the effect is likely to be most important in the class of crime committed by professional criminals where the police are most in danger. Such a view has been borne out by high police officials both in England and in Canada. The Commissioner of Police of London, England, in his evidence before the Royal Commission on Capital Punishment, told of [a gang of armed robbers who continued operations after one of their members was sentenced to death and his sentence commuted to penal servitude for life; but disbanded and disappeared when, on a later occasion, two others were convicted and hanged.] In a recent statement, former Royal Canadian Mounted Police Commissioner L. H. Nicholson declared in the **Ottawa Citizen** that the death penalty should be retained in Canada, particularly to safeguard society against vicious criminal types. "It would not be an exaggeration to say the criminal fraternity generally would welcome abolition of capital punishment," Mr. Nicholson said.[4]

In the debate on capital punishment in the British House of Commons in February, 1955, the Home Secretary gave three reasons why the Government was opposed to abolition. The first of them was that the Government was not disposed to reject the evidence of many experienced persons that the death penalty is a unique deterrent to professional criminals. Secondly the British Government pointed out that the alternative to execution, namely imprisonment for life, gave rise to serious difficulty. Where and for how long should we imprison the convicted muderer? The imprisoned murderer has everything to gain and nothing to lose by murdering his guards. Why should a murderer who has once been convicted of that offence be given the opportunity to add a second victim to his list? The British Parliament got round this difficulty by retaining the death penalty for second convictions of murder and thus in principle really accepted the case for capital punishment. The British Government's third and last reason against abolition was their conviction that it would be wrong to abolish the death penalty unless there was a clearly overwhelming public sentiment in favour of change, and they rightly believed that the contrary was the case. Such in fact has proved to be the case. As in New Zealand so now in Britain the issue of capital punishment has become a burning political issue, as indeed it should.

Actually, the argument based upon statistics would seem to be best left out of the discussion as both sides can make the figures support their own case. Indeed such an arithmetical argument is surely utterly irrelevant to the basic issue involved in any given murder; namely that Justice be done. What is at stake when a criminal is charged with "wilfully and of his malice aforethought, killing" another human being is not deterrence at all, but that just retribution be meted out to the criminal IF his guilt can be established beyond a reasonable doubt.

To think of capital punishment merely in terms of such deterrence is surely to make complete nonsense of the first principles of natural justice and the moral law. By taking such a mundane yardstick as utility in this matter, and making that the crux of their position, the abolitionists have in fact reduced justice to a mere department of economics. That deterrence has, in fact, become the chief consideration in the modern discussion of this question is really only a measure of how debased modern ideas of Law and Justice have fallen. It merely reflects the sloppy "positivistic," "relativistic" and "scientistic" notions of human nature, conduct and destiny that are in vogue today. If we are to think clearly about this question we must stop asking ourselves whether capital punishment deters, and, instead, ask the question: given the fact that an individual has wilfully taken a human life, is it just, or is it not just for society to demand the supreme penalty of the law? Does the murderer or does he not deserve to give his life in exchange?

For thousands of years the great majority of civilized mankind have answered that Justice herself requires that we answer both questions in the affirmative. Yes! It is just that the killer must himself be killed, not merely to deter others—that would be to treat him as a mere means to some other end —but to restore the just order which he has made unstable by his bloody deed. However much our so-called "progressive" thinkers may dislike to face the fact, capital punishment is essentially retributive justice.

For that matter, all and ANY punishment is also retributive justice, and cannot morally be justified on any other grounds. If you rule out the idea of just desert and retribution for wrong doing and leave only deterrence as a valid ground for punishment, there is no reason whatsoever why you should confine yourself to inflicting pain upon the actual doer of the wrong deed; why you should not, for example, inflict pain upon his children and wife. That might well serve as the best deterrent of all, as the Nazis and Communists have so well proved when they confine a man's loved ones in a concentration camp. Yet such a proposal has only to be suggested in English speaking lands to excite a cry of horror and moral outrage. But why? The answer is, because it would be hard if not downright unfair that those who had done nothing wrong to deserve it should be made to suffer. Precisely. Such an answer implies that the connection of appropriateness in justice between wrong conduct and suffering must be there as well in order to make us acquiesce in the deterrence. Why we do NOT mind a burglar or one who assaults little girls being subjected to the inconvenience of imprisonment is that, whatever our professed theory of punishment may be, we feel that he deserves it. And that is the main reason why capital punishment has been demanded and maintained in Canada, because according to the most recent Gallup Poll taken in 1958 it is still felt by 52% of the adult Canadian population that the murderer is a person who deserves to be killed, and it is felt he deserves it because the majority of Canadians are still subconsciously thinking and feeling in terms of Christian rather than so called "scientific" ideas and emotions.

So far from the Christian Church having been opposed to the death penalty for murder, the FACT is that it was the Church which introduced capital punishment into the legal codes of the Western states. As the Church began to exercise more influence in the affairs of the barbarian nations which succeeded the Roman Empire in the West, so the Christian understanding of personal status and of the sanctity of innocent human life became to an increasing extent the norm both of law and of economic affairs. This may not be equated, however, quite simply with a steady humanizing of justice.

The treatment of murder, in contrast with that accorded to it in old Germanic and Anglo-Saxon law, is a case in point. In old Germanic law it was possible to provide Wergild or man price as a positive expiation of the crime of murder. Then, thanks to the influence of the Christian Church, the death of a person came to be regarded as so grave an offence that it could only be expiated by the death of the killer. In other words, it was no longer possible to get away with murder by making a simple money payment in exchange for the human life destroyed. According to Professors H. H. Schrey, H. Walz, and Whitehouse, in their book THE BIBLICAL DOCTRINE OF JUSTICE—

It was the personal worth accorded to a man which accounted for the change, but the effect in this case was to produce a more severe penalty than was envisaged in Germanic law.[5]

It was precisely because the Church took such a serious view of the sanctity of innocent human life that it demanded of the secular power that the punishment inflicted for murder should adequately reflect the revulsion felt by Christian society against murder most foul. The Church assigns a special value to the life of man because he was created in the image of God. He is not only like God in the essential elements of his nature, but he is God's vicegerent upon earth. Any indignity or injury inflicted on a human being is thus an act of irreverence towards God. Deliberate destruction of this image of God is not only an act of rebellion against God's sovereignty but an assault on the life of God in man, for which no punishment can be too drastic. Hence the Divine Command given to mankind after the Great Deluge—

Whoso sheddeth man's blood, by man shall his blood be shed, for in the image of God made He man. (Genesis, chapter nine, verse six.)

As a violation of the Commandment "Thou shalt love thy neighbour as thyself," the crime of murder is in a unique category, because as far as this world is concerned, there is no way of being reconciled to the victim of a murder, and no possibility of securing the victim's forgiveness. That is why in no other crime in Biblical jurisprudence do we have the penalty assigned for the reason that man is made in the image of God. Such a consideration is reserved for murder alone. The reason assigned for the death penalty is still valid, since man is still created in God's image.

At this point it will be asked, What about the Sixth Commandment? Does this not annul the death penalty for murder? The answer is that it does not. According to the best Hebrew and Greek scholars this text in the original tongues reads "Thou shalt NOT murder" and not as abolitionists falsely sup-

pose "Thou shall not kill." When our Lord quotes the
Sixth Commandment He uses the term "murder" in
all three accounts, Matthew, Mark and Luke. All
killing is NOT murder any more than all sexual in-
tercourse is adultery. According to the teaching of
Holy Scripture it is possible and lawful under certain circumstances to take human life without com-
mitting murder. That the Sixth Commandment has
in view violent, wilful, malicious and premeditated
assault upon human life is made clear by the merciful provision of cities of refuge to which the person
guilty of manslaughter might flee. This institution
of cities of refuge, an account of which may be
found in Numbers chapter 35 and Joshua chapter
20, demanded that a strict discrimination be made
between accidental homicide and wilful murder.

In those olden times there were no policemen to
run down the murderer, so the next of kin was made
the "avenger of blood." Upon hearing that his near
relative had been slain, he was duty bound under
the Mosaic Law to pursue the killer the moment he
heard of the killing, and to slay the murderer on
sight. There was one difficulty, however, which
had to be faced then as it has to be faced now. Suppose the killing was accidental? The slayer did it unintentionally or as the Revised Version states in the
Book of Joshua "unwittingly." In such cases of accidental death the slayer was judged innocent and
rightly given sanctuary in one of the cities of refuge
where the avenger of blood was not permitted to
touch him. In British criminal law, cases of manslaughter likewise came to be distinguished from

cases of wilful murder. Thus both Hebrew and British criminal law have distinguished between wilful homicide and accidental death and judicial execution of convicted murderers. It is the sanctity of innocent human life that underlies the Sixth Commandment and not any intention to annul capital punishment.

Granting such a distinction between judicial execution and wilful homicide, it may be asked, Is it not the duty of Christians to forgive those who trespass against them? The answer to this question is that according to Christ's teaching we can only forgive those who have wronged us personally. Only God can forgive the murderer for his great trespass, since the one person who COULD FORGIVE HIM IS DEAD. For anyone else including the State to forgive the murderer would be the height of blasphemy and presumption, since God alone has the moral authority to forgive ALL men of their sins. Indeed it was for claiming to forgive men their sins that Christ was executed by the Jewish authorities. Jesus claimed to have God's authority to say to the sick of the palsy, "Arise, take up thy bed and walk; thy sins are forgiven thee." Now it is quite natural and proper for a man to forgive something you do to HIM. Thus if somebody cheats me out of $20.00 it is quite possible and reasonable for me to say, "Well, I forgive him, we will say no more about it." But what would you say if somebody had done YOU out of $20.00 and I said, "That's all right. I forgive him on YOUR behalf"?

What applies in the case of trying to forgive the murderer also applies to the attempt to reform him and "redeem" him. How can the murderer be reformed if he is executed, ask the abolitionists. Is not the main purpose of punishment to reform criminals? According to the traditional teachings of the Church no punishment is defensible either as a deterrent or as a remedial measure, unless it is first recognized as being JUST and therefore RETRIBUTIVE but not vindictive in character. Those who have become foreign to good to the point of trying to spread evil cannot be reinstated in good except by the imposition of some suffering and pain upon their OWN bodies. Such suffering must be inflicted upon the criminal until the remnants of humanity and decency inside him are awakened and he cries out in astonishment, "Why do others thus harm me?" Thus the primary purpose of punishment is NOT TO REFORM the criminal but to get him to repent of his evil deed and admit that he has done wrong and justly deserves his punishment. Without such a sense of just desert no so called "reformative treatment" could have the slightest effect upon the criminal. Thus chastisement is uniquely a process of providing pure good to men who do NOT want it, and a method of arousing in criminals the desire for pure good through suffering or even through death.

As St. Augustine made quite clear, the state, so far from being an instrument of human emancipation from sin and the perfectibility of criminals, is merely a strait jacket for human sinfulness, to be justified at best as a divinely appointed means of restraining sin, while the Church gets on with the business of mediating to mankind the grace and love of God which alone can redeem and "reform" men of their sins.[6] The right Christian thing to do if one had committed a murder would be to give oneself up to the police and be hanged. Before one was hanged he could repent of his evil deed and then go to meet his Maker with a clear conscience knowing that God had forgiven him as He forgave the dying thief upon his cross. It is for this reason that in all Christian states a chaplain has been provided at executions. Thus the condemned murderer has the opportunity, if he so desires, to make his peace with his Maker—a very essential grace not usually given to his victim "cut off even in the blossom of his sin."

In spite of tons of rationalist and secular propaganda, this conviction, that punishment in general and capital punishment in particular is just retribution for the disturbance of the social order, still holds good amongst most ordinary Canadians. By his verdict, the judge restores the just order which has become unstable. The man who has been robbed has his property returned to him, he who had lost his good name receives it back again. Thus a judicial sentence is essentially a process of restoration. From this point of view, we can see that the most ancient rule of criminal law, the *Jus Talionis,* an eye for an eye and a tooth for a tooth, has a profound meaning. Fundamentally the act of judicial judgment is an act of restoration; the return to its right place. The injured party receives back what was taken from him. There are, however, cases in which this direct restoration is not possible. The lost eye cannot be restored to its socket. Therefore instead of actual restoration, of the restitution which is not possible, there is a representative symbolic restoration. The injurer is made equal to the injured by the infliction of an equivalent injury, and thus the social equilibrium, the just order is restored. The wrong doer who cannot make his actual injury good now receives his just due in the form of a just penalty, that is a penalty corresponding to the injury. Thus the primary idea of justice in punishment is seen to be equivalence, the balance of guilt or injury with satisfaction and atonement. That alone is the meaning of the falsely decried terms, "retribution," "atonement," "satisfaction."[7]

Hence it is entirely fallacious to discredit retributive punishment by connecting it—still more by identifying it—with the motive of revenge. We can only admit the connection if we also recognize in vengeance an impulse to restore a disturbed order, an impulse which may be obscured by passion, but which has an objective basis in Justice. By punishment, things are replaced in their right order; the advantage which the wrongdoer has unlawfully acquired is taken from him; the injury suffered by society is repaired. Accordingly retributive punishment is not in any way subjective in character, but purely objective. The mechanisms of a British or Canadian court are deliberately made impersonal precisely to avoid any personal feelings of antagonism and revenge. Such a court simply accords to a man what he has earned and BROUGHT UPON HIMSELF BY HIS OWN CONDUCT.

It is this sense of just retribution for wrong-doing which underlies the New Testament conception of punishment. As St. Paul warns us—

Be not deceived; God is not mocked; for whatsoever a man soweth, that shall he also reap. (Galatians 6:7.)

If God were to let wrong doing go unpunished it would mean that His moral order had no force, and that He did not take His own commandments seriously. The just judgment of God, by which a man reaps what he has sown, is unshakably founded on the idea of God's Holiness and Righteousness. (Matthew 21:40; 22:13.)

According to the New Testament, God's Justice should be the prototype of all earthly criminal justice, and if the earthly state does in fact reflect such divine justice in its positive laws, then the Church calls upon all her members to obey the laws of the earthly state as a matter of conscience.

God's Justice has in fact been the yardstick by which fundamental British and Canadian criminal law have up till now been structured and operated. God alone is the Sovereign Ruler of our British Realms as is classically revealed in the Coronation Service. Our beloved and gracious Queen at her enthronement in Westminster Abbey was anointed with Holy Oil by the Archbishop of Canterbury in exactly the same way as the Kings of Israel and Judah were anointed with oil by the High Priests and Prophets, signifying that she rules as God's earthly vicegerent. Likewise she was presented with a copy of the Holy Bible with these striking words—

Our Gracious Queen, we present you with this Book, the most valuable thing that this world affords. Here is wisdom; this is the Royal Law; these are the lively oracles of God.

She was then asked to take her Oath of Office and asked if she would obey them. Only when she had answered in the affirmative did the ceremony proceed.

The whole Coronation Service is an outward and visible sign of the linking of our British Kingdoms and Commonwealth with the Kingdom of our Lord and of His Christ. It is the most solemn expression of our historic British belief that the true and only source of all human government and political power lies in God. For God alone is the ground and origin of government. Our British states are under God's rule. Thus the Coronation Service is a living parable of St. Paul's idea that "there is no power or authority except from God." God is the source and therefore the limit of the Canadian Cabinet's authority. A government which invests itself with absolute powers over its citizens is by this doctrine condemned as immoral and not worthy of men's allegiance. God has thus entrusted to Her Majesty and all her agents such coercive powers as are necessary to hold the forces of evil and injustice in men's hearts in check, while the Church gets on with the business of teaching the Queen's subjects around the world a better and a higher law of grace and love. If Canadians did of their own free will what God's Justice requires, there would of course be no need of a criminal law and penal system. As long as evil continues in Canada so long will the strong arm of Her Majesty's police forces be required to deal with it.

Thus the main function of all British states is the administration of criminal justice, which in turn is based in our British lands upon the presumption of a Moral Order which must not be infringed, and the infringement of which requires restitution, atonement and punishment.[8]

According to historic British political doctrine the State is NOT the ultimate form of community but merely the divinely ordained instrument for regulating the relations of what St. Augustine calls the exterior man. In other words the role of the State is purely FORMAL; as such, it can punish men for proven offences against the Law. It CANNOT possibly "reform" or "rehabilitate" criminals.

It is for such reasons that both our Lord and St. Paul teach us that the powers that be in government over men wield the sword as "holy servants" of God. The State, that is to say, is a divinely ordained instrument for the restraint NOT the reform of evil, and even its normal system of penalties and sanctions including the use of the sword are God ordained. (John 19:11; Mark 12:17; Romans 13:1-7.) Our Lord's acknowledgement that Caesar and Pilate have a legitimate place in the control of human society could have had little reality in it, unless it also involved a measure of approval of some of the sanctions employed by Roman administrators to maintain justice and order, including the use of the sword in the execution of murderers.

Not only did Jesus thus give assent to non-love methods in Roman secular rule, He also accepted the framework of the Jewish civil administration, conducted by the local synagogue court and the Jewish Sanhedrin, operated on the basis of the Mosaic Law. This Jewish Law consisted not merely in provisions for religious observance; much of it regulated purely secular affairs, prescribing coercive sanctions, including violent physical penalties for its enforcement. The compilers and administrators of this Mosaic Law saw well enough that even in a theocracy there were rogues as well as righteous, and that rogues needed to be treated with rigour. As administered in the time of Christ, the penalties inflicted under this Law and the customary procedure which had gathered around it included imprisonment, scourging, and capital punishment by stoning.

While Jesus certainly pleaded for humaneness in applying the Law, there is NO evidence that He repudiated the Mosaic Law as such nor that He suggested basic changes in the procedure of these Jewish Courts. In fact He did not even repudiate the principle of the *Lex Talionis* at this SECULAR LEVEL. In St. Mark chapter VII, 9-13 He is said to refer to the Law's penalty of death for evil speech against parents as the "commandment of God." In Matthew chapter V, 21ff, He alludes to death for murder apparently as a punishment which still stands.[9]

While claiming authority to amend this Jewish legal and moral code, Jesus, be it observed, never amends it by way of relaxation, never saying that

God required less than the Old Law said, but by tightening up, declares that God requires much more. Not only the act of murder, but even the wish to murder, if indulged in and allowed to go on ministering to lethal desires, would bring a man to Hell, where the worm died not, and the fire was not quenched.

For St. Paul the State does properly and rightly exactly the opposite of what the individual Christian is to do; it takes vengeance on him who does evil. Thus St. Paul writes (Romans chapter 13:3-4) —

Rulers are not a terror to them who do good works, but only to evil. For he is a holy servant of God to thee for good; but if thou do that which is evil, be afraid, for he beareth not the sword in vain; for he is a holy servant of God, a revenger to execute wrath upon him that doeth evil.

And yet St. Paul also tells us that the Christian on the contrary is by no means to repay evil with evil. Yet as Christians we are to submit ourselves to the State for conscience's sake. For if the State takes vengeance upon the evil doer it does so as God's servant. Even if it does not know this itself, it stands nevertheless unconsciously in God's service.[9]

How may we explain this contradiction between the State using force and power and the Christian being told by St. Paul to rely upon persuasion and love? The tensions between the State's concern with the judicial principle of the retribution of evil doing and the Christian's concern for the forgiveness of wrongs done personally to himself is due to the chronological tension which characterizes the New

Testament situation; that is, the fact that God's Rule of Love has already begun in Christ, and yet its final consummation is nevertheless still outstanding. God's great D-Day has taken place in the person of His Son, Christ, but His V-J Day is still to come when Christ will have triumphed over all the forces of evil at work in this world.

When and where then did the idea ever arise that capital punishment is "judicial savagery," "primitive retaliation" and a brutalizing form of deliberate vengeance? According to the celebrated historian of Western social thought, William Lecky, the answer is that the movement for abolition arose out of the great 18th Century revolution in human thought known as the so-called European Enlightenment. Thus Lecky says:—

The reform of the law in England, as over the rest of Europe, may ultimately be traced to that Voltarian school of which Beccaria was the chief representative, for the impulse created by his treatise "On Crime and Punishment" was universal, and it was the first great effort to infuse a spirit of philanthropy into the penal code, making it a main object of legislation to inflict the smallest amount of suffering. Beccaria is especially identified with the cause of the abolition of capital punishment.[10]

For these persons, belief in God is an unnecessary hypothesis. Led by Voltaire and Rousseau in France, Vico and Beccaria in Italy, Savigny, Marx and Kelsen in Germany, Hume and Bentham in England, Franklin and Paine in America, there arose a concerted attack upon the whole Christian basis of

European civilization, including our whole Western conception of the place of Justice and Morality in the punishment of crime. The accepted legal norms and the moral values upon which they were based were all called in question, derided, and thrown away as medieval and barbaric. Henceforth the value of man, and the meaning of his history as well as the legal norms and social values by which man should live, are all to be found in what man is IN and FOR himself, rather than in the nature of a Just and Holy God and of what man is worth to God. Man can redeem himself by scientific method applied to his social life, rather than by repentance of his sins and by relying upon God's grace to sweeten human relationships. As Condorcet put it in his oration upon his reception into the French Academie of Sciences, a new race of social scientists would arise to whom physical and social phenomena would appear in the same light, because "Strangers to our race, they would study human society as we study those of the beavers and the bees." And although Condorcet admits that this is an unattainable ideal because the observer is himself part of human society, he still exhorts the scholars "to introduce into the moral sciences the philosophy and method of the natural sciences."[11]

This mighty movement to secularize and to "scientize" the whole basis of Western civilization could not but have profound effects upon traditional ideas of Law and Justice and of justice in punishment. Whilst in the previous 2000 years the spiritual and political leaders of European society had believed in the existence of an objective order of Justice and Morality, and had regarded all legal systems as a continuing advance towards Justice, there now arose under the leadership of Friedrich Karl von Savigny a new conception of Law. It arose out of the new science devoted to historical legal research. From that moment all discussion of Justice as the source and essence of Law, and of an Eternal Moral Law for all men, abruptly disappeared from the Continent. Why? The answer is that these "positive" lawyers, as they were pleased to call themselves, managed to drive a fatal wedge between criminal justice and the Natural Moral Law, between the legal systems of the various states of Western Europe and Christian morality as understood by the Western Church for a thousand years.

The thin end of this wedge to detach the idea of justice entirely from its theological context and religious roots was the theory that because all human laws vary so much from place to place and from time to time, they must all be considered purely relative and therefore changeable. In the light of such diversity not one of the countless laws past or present could any longer be deemed unquestionably based upon divine and changeless principles of Justice. Since such principles were thought to have been proved never to have been operative, Justice from that moment ceased to be revered as an end in itself. Instead of having a timelessly valid justice for ALL men there now arose the so-called more "scientific" view of law as the mere product of historical growth and change. Justice now took a rank below any positive system of Law, and it became degraded into an instrument which any individual state could wield for the purpose of carrying out its own designs.

When such relativistic ideas of law were combined with 19th Century scientific materialism, evolutionary utopianism and the liberal doctrine of progress, it is not suprising that the traditional Western and Christian idea of Justice and of such Justice in punishment was stripped of all divine sanction and dignity. Henceforth the terrible idea began to spread through the law schools of Europe and North America that, in the English jurist Austin's words:

Law is the Command of the Sovereign Power in the State.[12]

That is to say, Austin separated ethics from the science of jurisprudence, holding that positive law is not something initially given by God and interpreted by man in the light of his reason and historical experience. On the contrary every positive law is:—

Set by a sovereign person or sovereign body of persons to a member or members of the independent political society wherein that person or body is sovereign or superior.

Positive law is such only by a sovereign's command. The sovereign is the person or persons whose commands are habitually obeyed by the great bulk of the community. In plain English this means that justice is no more than conformity with the rules laid down by the Government or class in power. By thus identifying law with the naked will of the legal sovereign, Austin in effect makes MIGHT INTO RIGHT, and justice the will of the stronger.

Given such ideas of law it is hardly surprising that the totalitarian state soon made its appearance upon the stage of world history, for such a state is merely the practical application of such a "scientific" view of law. Having abolished the Law and Justice of Almighty God as a criterion of human law and justice in punishment, it is not surprising that such secular states as Napoleon's France, Hitler's Germany and Stalin's Russia felt quite justified in assuming that they were sovereign, in the sense of not being limited by any higher power. Hitler never acted illegally after he came to power. By the Empowering Act of March 23, 1933, Hitler was given the legal right to alter or suspend certain articles in the German constitution; by a further law in the following year he was given authority to frame new constitutional law. In fact, the will of the Fuhrer became the source of law in Germany. He acted always within the constitution. And yet it is not in dispute that his advent to power marked the end of the reign of law as it had been known in Western Europe. Not only clergy but every Christian citizen is in duty bound to protest if the lawyers in our universities teach that law may be defined without reference to Justice, as the will of the contemporary sovereign power.

Thus such purely utilitarian considerations as "deterrence" and the "rehabilitation" of the offender began to replace the well-tried conception of "punishment" and "just retribution of criminals proved guilty of crime."

In a recent address in the House of Commons the

Minister of Justice gave an outline of government policy which is a portent of things to come:—

We are attempting to develop a scientific and socially adequate system of penology in Canada, one designed to serve the best interests of society and to keep our prison population to a minimum . . . and to ensure that men committed to prison receive the type of consideration, education, handling and rehabilitation training that they need and which is designed to return them as quickly as possible as useful members of society.[13]

As Professor Bienenfeld well says, writing of these trends in his great work THE RECOVERY OF JUSTICE:—

With the breakdown in men's belief in justice, the ominous doctrine of the Power State was born, and when the Bismarck government adopted it theory turned into tragic practice. It was that spiritual catastrophe, that collapse of the belief in eternal justice, that conception of the amoral and ruthless state, which sowed the seeds of the First and Second World Wars, changed solemn agreements into scraps of paper and eventually reduced Europe to a desert.[14]

According to this so-called sociological theory of law, first propounded by Chief Justice Holmes and Thomas Dewey and now advocated by Roscoe Pound and Julius Stone, the judge's task is really only a form of social engineering. The law is essentially relative to social interests, to expediency, to compromise, and its main function is the avoidance of social friction. It is therefore an experimental science, rather than one concerned with first principles. The law is merely what the courts decide to do, and therefore the study of the law becomes simply a scientific observation of the way courts actually behave in response to cases brought before them. Such legal behaviourism surely leaves out from the law the function of guiding the judge as to how he OUGHT to decide a case, and accordingly deprives the judge also of any grounds on which he could seek such guidance in his efforts to reach a just decision. By thus ignoring the ultimate principles upon which the day-to-day operation of the courts should be based, this sociological school of law is also in grave danger of destroying our respect for the Law altogether. Justice is surely more than a device for the avoidance of social friction.

As the British theologian Professor N. Micklem points out:—

The engineer's task is to tinker with the car to make it go; but it will not run for long or securely apart from the due observation of the fundamental principles of mechanics with which he may not tinker. Jurisprudence may be in large measure an empirical science, but it has transcendental postulates or principles. The avoidance of reference to the transcendental or spiritual in this sociological theory leads to very great obscurity.[15]

At present the main function of the law courts in this country is to determine whether or not persons accused of crime committed the act in question. Such psychological considerations as motive are taken into account only when they have a bearing on the probability or improbability of guilt, or in murder cases where insanity can be pleaded.

Our present legal system is based on the Christian assumptions: first, that everybody, except children and lunatics, knows the difference between right and wrong; secondly, that everybody apart from the same two exceptions is able to choose between doing right and wrong; and lastly, that anyone who chooses to do wrong should be properly punished for it.

Now it seems that the abolitionists would like us all to accept the theories of psychology and penology. We are to believe that the murderer is nothing but the product of his heredity acting upon his environment, and that he has gone wrong because he has failed to adjust himself properly to his society. Crime is not the result of sinfulness but of sickness. Thus the criminal, including the murderer, should be treated in a hospital rather than punished in a prison. As Mr. Gerald Wright, Chief Inspector of Reform Institutions for Ontario says:

The traditional process of trial, conviction and punishment is archaic, and no longer compatible with enlightened sociological thinking . . . It is our conviction that a sentence can no longer be regarded as a substitute for diagnosis. We contend that as most serious offences are symptomatic of social or psychological aberrations, the treatment of the offender should be determined by a diagnostic investigation, which should be an integral part of the treatment process, COMMENCING BEFORE TRIAL and ending with the ultimate emancipation of the offender from his criminality.[16]

Up till now Canadian criminal law has refused to

define anti-social conduct as due to sickness. On the contrary it maintains that an intelligible division can be made between those who are mentally sick and those who are plain wicked. A line can be drawn between those whose offences are explained by illness and those who cannot legitimately plead ill-health as mitigation of, or excuse for, their criminal conduct but must shoulder responsibility for their own actions. Of this attempt to define the limits within which mental incapacity undermines criminal responsibility the most famous is the formula embodied in the McNaghten Rules which still govern American and British law. By this a man is held to be responsible for his actions unless he is "labouring under such a defect of reason, from disease of the mind, as not to know the nature and quality of the act he was doing, or if he did know it, that he did not know he was doing what was wrong."[17]

This formula applies, in principle, to responsibility for criminal acts of every kind and it has even been used in civil cases.

Whether applied to criminal or civil matters, the McNaghten formula is essentially a test of responsibility.

If it could be shown that some deviant conduct is due to an INDEPENDENTLY ascertainable mental disorder we could no doubt distinguish between those who are responsible and those who are not responsible for their acts. Unfortunately, as Mrs. Barbara Wootton has proved in her recent book SOCIAL SCIENCE AND SOCIAL PATHOLOGY, this is well-nigh impossible, because the criminal conduct in question is all too often a main element in the definition of the disease itself. The selfish fellow who cannot be deterred from misbehaving behaves as he does because he is judged a "psychopath," but he is judged a "psychopath" because he behaves as he does. Thus she writes:—

The psychopath is a critical case for those who would retain a distinction between the responsible and the irresponsible. For, as Professor Lewis himself has admitted, the psychopath makes nonsense of every attempt to distinguish the sick from the healthy delinquent by the presence or absence of a psychiatric syndrome, or by symptoms of mental disorder which are INDEPENDENT OF HIS OBJECTIONABLE BEHAVIOUR. In his case no such symptoms can be diagnosed because it is just the absence of them which causes him to be classified as psychopathic. He is in fact, par excellence, *the model of the circular process by which mental abnormality is inferred from anti-social behaviour, while anti-social behaviour is explained by mental abnormality.*[18]

Such is the scientific basis of the penological system Mr. Fulton and Mr. Wright would have us adopt, a system which depends upon a tautology! Such people whom Mr. Wright classifies as psychopaths used to be thought extremely wicked. Today we are asked to classify them as cases of mental disorder. Paradoxically, this has the strange effect that, if you are consistently wicked enough, you may hope to be excused for your misdeeds; but if your wickedness is only moderate, or if you show occasional signs of repentance or reform, then you must expect to take the blame for what you do, and perhaps also be punished for it. It is for this reason that Barbara Wootton says:—

So illogical a position can hardly, one would think, prove tenable for long. Hence the psychopath may well prove to be the thin end of the wedge which will ultimately shatter the whole idea of moral responsibility as a factor in the treatment of anti-social personalities.[19]

Let us admit the truth. The criminal does what he does because he is what he is. The only problem is: how can we get him to behave differently?

The answer is that we can PUNISH him until such time as he chooses to amend his naughty ways. Better still, we can try to inculcate our citizens while they are young in Christian values, give them every opportunity to develop all their talents, and then punish them if they prefer to break the law of the land when they grow up.

According to Dr. Bernard Glueck, the Supervising Psychiatrist of Sing Sing Prison:—

The problem would be eased, and certainly the question of responsibilty would not have to be raised, if the concept of management of the anti-social individual were changed from that of punishment as the main instrument of control, to a concept of the anti-social individual as a sick person, in need of treatment rather than punishment.[20]

The great strength of the McNaghten formula is that it does provide a criterion for distinguishing between the guilty and the crazy which is independent of anybody's criminal conduct. A man's capacity for understanding can be tested in various ways, and it is demonstrated in many aspects of his behaviour. This criterion, moreover, is not only intelligible to laymen not learned in the Law but it also satisfies certain elementary requirements of justice. It provides a safe and common-sensical definition of the minimum group about whose inclusion in the category of irresponsibles there can be no dispute. You cannot really blame a madman who does not know what he is doing.

The great weakness of any alternatives based on the theory that ALL crime is a disease rather than an expression of plain human wickedness is that we have to decide who can help doing what. Just where do we draw the line between those who are so sick that they commit foul murders and those who are only a little sick so that they steal?

Are we going to let the psychiatrists do for our morals and penal laws what Darwin and Huxley did for our pedigree, or are we going to remain true to our noble Christian past by which we learned to stop behaving like monkeys and try to live as responsible persons made in the image of Almighty God.

References and Notes

1. A. V. Dicey, Law of the Constitution, 8th ed., 1931, p. 207. Macmillan.
2. G. Gardiner, Capital Punishment as a Deterrent, Gollancz. Ernest Gowers, A Life for a Life, Chatto and Windus. A. Koestler. Reflections on Hanging. Gollancz.
3. Royal Commission on Capital Punishment, 1949-53. Report HMSO Cmd 8932.
4. Quoted, Ottawa Citizen, Jan. 25th 1960.
5. H. Schrey, H. Walz, W. A. Whitehouse, The Biblical Doc-

trine of Justice and Law, p. 155ff. SCM Press, London, 1955.

6. C. N. Cochrane, Christianity and Classical Culture, Preface, OUP, 1944.

7. Emil Brunner, Justice and the Social Order, pp. 194-198. Lutterworth, London, 1945.

8. Moral Basis of Burke's Political Thought, C. Parkin, CUP '56.

9. Oscar Cullman, The State in the New Testament, pp.50-70. SCM 1957. J. C. Bennett, Christians and the State, Scribners 1959.

10. W. Lecky, The Rise and Influence of Rationalism in Europe, Vol. One, p. 349. Longmans Green and Co., London, 1910.

11. F. A. Hayek, The Counter-Revolution of Science, pp. 107-9. The Free Press, Glencoe, Illinois, 1952. D. R. G. Owen, Scientism, Man and Religion, pp. 54-72. A brilliant discussion of sociological scientism. Westminster Press, 1952.

12. Lord Lochee, Encyclopaedia Britannica, 11th edition, New York, 1911, pp. 571-3 for an excellent treatment of Austin's theory of law.

13. Report of the Council for Social Service, quoting p. 30, 1959.

14. F. R. Bienenfeld, Rediscovery of Justice, pp. 14-16, George Allen, 1947.

15. N. Micklem, THE LAW and the Laws. Chap. Seven, 60-65, Sweet and Maxwell, London, 1953. See also A. P. D'Entreves Natural Law. Hutchinson.

16. Gerald Wright, quoted by United Church Observer, Jan. 15th, 1960, p. 6.

17. Royal Commission on Capital Punishment, p. 79. London.

18. Lady Barbara Wootton. Social Science and Social Pathology, p. 250. Allen and Unwin, 1959. This book is a trenchant criticism of all modern theories of the cause of crime and should be compulsory reading for all politicians and clergy in Canada.

19. Ibid, pp. 251ff.

20. Bernard Glueck, quoted by Wootton, ibid, p. 248.

See also Lord Pakenham, The Causes of Crime: The Roots of Crime, edited by East. Butterworth Press; Gregory Zilboorg, The Psychology of the Criminal Act and Punishment, Hogarth Press. The Roots of Crime. E. Glover, 1960. Isaiah Berlin. Two Concepts of Freedom.

I also refer the reader to my article entitled "A Secular Revolution in Christian Disguise," which appeared in the Canadian Bar Journal, August, 1958, and in His Dominion, November, 1958.

III

Capital Punishment
. . . Right and Necessary

by

G. Aiken Taylor

The current all-out campaign to abolish capital punishment is a rather curious phenomenon of our age—curious because it is not only world-wide (every country has its agitators against the death penalty) but also because it does not reflect any single religion or culture.

Whether in Indonesia, Ghana or the U. S.; whether among Moslems, Buddhists or avowed atheists—forces are being marshalled against capital punishment with equal enthusiasm. The Indian government has under advisement a measure outlawing the death penalty. Even Soviet Russia has abolished capital punishment for other than "political" crimes.

Obviously, therefore, one must look beyond the religious angle to understand why so many people representing so many different viewpoints should suddenly consider it barbarous to punish human beings with death.

The overture approved by the 1960 Presbyterian General Assembly, which has resulted in the report of the Christian Relations Committee to the 1961 Assembly, spoke of "sociological" and "humanitarian" considerations as well as the "guidance to be had from the Scriptures." Quite evidently, social considerations in this matter have been placed on a par with any religious considerations.

Sociologically the campaign probably reflects the universal revulsion most people feel at the wholesale killing which has been going on for too many centuries. Buddhists, Hindus and Christians alike are weary of man's demonstrated inhumanity to man. Thus the interest of abolitionists of capital punishment may partly be explained as a reaction against killing in general.

The educator may have another interest in the matter. Certain modern philosophies of education advance the theory that education and environment are able to accomplish those reforms for which punishment has traditionally been meted out. In other words it is popularly believed that the best way to stop crime and lawlessness is to educate the criminal; that punishment does no good.

A great deal is being written today against the principle of punishment *as such*. Penalties of any kind—these authors claim—are valid only if they effect the rehabilitation of the criminal. The aim of Justice—it is said—is to reconcile and redeem. Quite obviously there is no reconciliation possible after capital punishment has been inflicted. And education never has a chance to "restore to society" the man whose sentence snuffs out his life.

Again, we seem to be living in a time when "life" is prized above all things: honor, virtue, patriotism, heroism . . . justice. Fewer and fewer moderns believe that life should be sacrificed (or taken) for any reason. We even see this reverence for physical life in the practice of medicine where the valid and fundamental duty to respect life has often been expanded into the obligation to keep soul and body together under any circumstances, at all costs, as long as possible, regardless of the pain or other consequences.

If "life" (human existence) is more to be desired than anything else in all the universe, there is obviously little justification for ever denying it. If man's inalienable and ultimate possession is his life, one might properly question the right of anyone to take it.

Within the Christian community (in addition to the other considerations, above) it is widely believed that the Christian "ethic" demands the abolition of capital punishment. Some Christian leaders declare that the New Testament modifies the Old Testament in this respect and that "Jesus Christ would have rejected capital punishment" (Charles L. Allen).

The report of the Christian Relations Committee does not go so far as to say that the New Testament corrects the old or that Christ would not have agreed with the Law (we still believe the Old Testament to be inspired). However, the report argues that the New Testament "ethic of love" effectively forbids capital punishment and that the process of rehabilitation which is "God's redemption" should not be denied any man.

It is possible that all of the premises upon which

the abolition of the death penalty is argued may be questioned.

To begin with, it is beside the point to contend that there has been entirely too much killing in the history of the world. There has indeed been too much unjustified killing, but if men continue to justify the death penalty by their actions and capital punishment is what they deserve, then capital punishment continues to be the answer regardless of the record of their ancestors.

Furthermore, there is no validity to the argument: "Capital punishment has not abolished murder so let's abolish capital punishment." This contention is first cousin to the argument: "Christianity has been in the world 2,000 years and it has not abolished sin, so let's abolish Christianity."

Sometimes the argument is advanced that "there is no substantial evidence that capital punishment has decreased crime anywhere at any time" (Charles L. Allen). That contention is amply covered by the minority report to this Assembly. It, too, is essentially a non-valid argument. It is much like saying: "There is no evidence that laws against stealing have reduced thievery." One can submit little evidence to that effect because there have always been laws against stealing. Moreover, despite man's larcenous nature, laws against stealing are still necessary . . . and good.

The popular notion that the answer to crime is better education exhibits two serious flaws:

1) It is not true that criminal tendencies are less observable among more educated people. Some of the most senseless and cruel crimes have been committed

by persons of highest education and advantages, witness the sensational Leopold and Loeb case of the 20's. And,

2) No Christian would contend that the answer to evil is education. The answer to evil is the grace of God or the restraining power of God: the one to regenerate, the other to control.

If we think that human passion and greed can be changed by precept and example we are strange Christians indeed. A man like Caryl Chessman, who thinks nothing of forcing unnatural sex acts upon kidnapped women—and who goes to his death sneering at God—is not changeable by pedagogy, precept or even punishment.

Most important of all, it is a serious mistake to assume that law and order prevails upon this troubled earth (that most people behave themselves) because they have a true, inner disposition to godliness and good behavior—that if the restraints imposed by police force or the threat of force were removed, people would still behave. Only a small percentage of any society gives evidence of being truly redeemed. Being Presbyterians we also believe that the percentage which gives evidence of being truly redeemed is the same percentage of those redeemable—that is of those who are ever going to be redeemed.

It seems hardly necessary, in other words, to argue that human behavior, generally speaking, is held in check not by conscience as much as by coercion: by laws, restraints and prohibition . . . in short by force or the fear of force. The fear which makes people behave may be simply fear of convention or of public displeasure, but it is, nevertheless, fear.

Punishment, however, is not administered solely as a deterrent to misbehavior. Punishment is primarily administered as a *penalty*: "For every action there is an equal and opposite reaction." The principle of penalty is an unalterable law of the universe: "The soul that sinneth it shall die." Someone has said, "You don't break God's laws; you violate God's laws and they break you!"

The person who commits a crime incurs a penalty. He is not simply liable to rehabilitation, he is subject to punishment. And this is true whether or not others may be deterred by what happens to him. If there is no penalty, if there is only rehabilitation and redemption, then crime is committed with impunity.

Let me make myself perfectly clear: A child, washing dishes in the sink, drops a dish and breaks it. You do not punish the child, you teach him how to wash dishes without breaking them. There is no penalty here, there is only "redemption." A teenager "borrows" a car and, being unskilled in driving, wrecks it. He didn't know what he was doing so he is better instructed, taught the danger of modern traffic and the reasons why high-powered machinery must be treated with respect. Again, there is no penalty, there is only "redemption." A young man goes berserk and from emotional instability and social maladjustment wreaks havoc in a neighborhood, perhaps killing a few people against whom he imagines that he has a "grudge." But his emotional instability and his social malajustment are blamed and he is placed under the care of a psychiatrist until he can be "restored safely to society." Again, there is no penalty, there is only "redemption."

But a society is sick, sick, sick which ignores or denies that a violation of fundamental law, a wrong done or crime committed, incurs a penalty as well as the privilege of rehabilitation. "Man is inclined to evil as the sparks fly upward." That evil issues in acts of evil against himself, against his neighbor and against God. Such evil sets in motion inexorable laws which are the very warp and woof of the universe: "For every action there is an equal and opposite reaction." And the reward of evil is not simply rehabilitation. Evil must first and foremost be *penalized* or Goodness is mocked.

God is interested in the salvation of evil men and Christ Jesus came to redeem sinners. But God's love and Christ's redemption do not overlook the necessity for a penalty. Our Lord's Atonement was first and foremost a satisfaction of divine justice— a coming to terms with the eternal penalty of sin.

Furthermore, the work of Christ Jesus was first and foremost an eternal redemption, not a temporal redemption. The liability always remains, even for the redeemed. When David sinned against God in the case of Uriah and Bathsheba, he found forgiveness. But the temporal liability remained and inexorably followed.

This brings us to the Christian perspective in the matter of punishment and, especially, capital punishment. This perspective includes 3 considerations: 1) What God commands, 2) What the Christian "ethic" demands, and 3) What is most desirable from the spiritual standpoint, relating to a sinner's salvation.

It should be recognized, at the outset, that most Christians tend to confuse the Christian personal ethic with the requirements of social order. In other words, we tend to apply what the Bible teaches us about how we—personally—should behave towards our neighbors with what the Bible teaches about how to preserve order in society. And there's a big difference.

As a Christian, I should adopt an attitude of charity towards the burglar who breaks into my home in the night and shoots me in the effort to escape. But it would obviously be foolish to apply the Christian personal principle of "turn the other cheek" to the problem of law enforcement. Only chaos would ensue if the state adopted a "forget it" attitude towards all who wanted to burglarize homes and shoot the occupants in the process. But what about capital punishment? It is the supreme "arm" of the state, the "queen" of penalties, so to speak, the ultimate "norm" of punishment, reflecting (as it does) God's judgment upon *all* sin of whatever kind.

Capital punishment is specifically enjoined in the Bible. "Whoso sheddeth man's blood, by man shall his blood be shed" (Gen. 9:6). This command is fully agreeable to the Sixth Commandment, "Thou shalt not kill" (Exodus 20:13), because the two appear in the same context. Exactly 25 verses after saying "Thou shalt not kill," the Law says, "He that smiteth a man so that he die, shall be surely put to death" (Exodus 2:12).

The Apostle Paul did not abrogate capital punish-
ent. When on trial, he insisted that if he had done
thing worthy of death he refused not to die!
cts 25:11). And in his famous essay on political
ory (Romans 13) he strongly supported the
wer of the sword" in the hand of the magistrate.

There is one final consideration from the Presby-
ian or Reformed viewpoint.

t is often argued that capital punishment re-
es the opportunity to reach a criminal for Christ.
e majority report of Christian Relations sug-
ts that we deny "God's redemption" to men who
put to death before they are rehabilitated.

Aside from the practical truth of the matter
ost condemned men turn to religion for the very
son that they are condemned) there are theologi-
considerations which make this argument a
ange one in the mouth of any Calvinist.

Presbyterians do not believe that man decides who
ll accept Christ and when. Presbyterians believe
at God Himself decides who will accept Christ and
en. No man ever cuts off another from eternal
demption by taking his life . . . before the Lord
d a fair chance to do anything with him. It would
t be mortally possible to send an unsaved man into
rnity whom God had marked for salvation. No
n frustrates the grace of God by denying to an-
her the possibility of "God's redemption" through
pital punishment.

That's the theology of it.

If capital punishment is no longer va
neither is the Sixth Commandment. They b
from the same Law.

Capital punishment is not abrogated in
Testament. In the Sermon on the Mou
Christ said that not a jot or tittle of the l
be changed by His coming—He came not to
but to fulfill (Matt. 5:17-18). As a matte
He increased the liability when He said that
the contemporary interpretation of the law
man into court for killing another, His in
tion of the Law made a man liable for simp
another.

You cannot argue that Jesus abrogated
ment because He often forgave. It was His
tive to forgive. But that prerogative is not
you and I share, for we are not God. And th
reference in the life and teachings of Jesu
effect that He abrogated the natural consequ
human misdeeds. The most famous illustrat
of the woman taken in adultery, is a case
You will find nothing in that story to sugg
He said to her accusers, "She does not deser
punished!"

The Lord Jesus died between two victims
ital punishment. And He, Himself, died a
of capital punishment. There is nothing in th
to suggest that had He been a blasphe
charged, and had He been fairly tried a
demned, He should not have been stoned.
cross, He saved the thief's soul. He did not '
him safely to society."

IV

The Keystone of
Our Penal System

by
T. ROBERT INGRAM

It is curious to be in the position of writing a piece in support of the power of the State of Texas to legislate and inflict the death penalty. It is like attempting to argue that human beings ought to have the power of speech. The fact is that just as human beings are those creatures of God who have the power of speech, so Texas and all other temporal governing authorities are realized in those human officials who have "the right of making laws with penalties of death, and consequently all less penalties . . . and of employing the force of the community in the execution of such laws."[1]

While John Locke's definition of political power is not offered as definitive because John Locke made it, clearly it is one of the best statements of a principle universally acknowledged and supported by individual powers of reason. Temporal power, political power, civil government, kingdom of the world, call it what you will, is that human agency properly authorized to inflict penalties of death and consequently all less penalties for the purpose of repairing broken laws. If there are to be laws by which men are governed, those laws must be enforced.

If laws can be broken with impunity, that is, without punishment, then the laws cease to exist as laws. If the power of a ruler (as distinguished from a father) to punish does not extend to the top—or head—or capital punishment of death, then it vanishes before the power of him who will resist punishment to the death. Failure to recognize that ultimate worldly power is the power to kill with impunity reflects an inability to comprehend the nature of power at all. Jesus told Pilate that if His kingdom were of this world, "then would my servants fight."[2]

There is today a concerted, highly organized, world-wide movement to "abolish" capital punishment. That movement is directed against what must be admitted to be the existing order, or the "status quo." "Abolition" (whatever it may turn out to mean) is therefore the innovation; as such, the burden of proof lies upon the advocates of abolition, not upon those who would support the created order of things. There is no burden of proof upon "those who claim the right on the part of the state to take life," as declared by Dr. John R. Silber in his article in the Texas Law Forum. The state is whoever or whatever has the right to take human life in punishment and war. Any effort to "abolish" that right or power is an effort to abolish the state itself: it is the definition of anarchy.

The proposals which purportedly would "abolish" capital punishment would not, of course, do so. They would simply declare, for what it may be worth, that the power to execute punishment is no longer vested in the legislative and judicial and executive machinery of the State of Texas. There is no attempt to say where that power is to be vested. Clearly it is an absurdity to "legislate" the "abolition" of the power to kill. That power is inherent in being alive: even animals and sharks can and do kill human beings. Men will still have the power to kill, whatever the professors may write about it. If no one has the right to kill in punishment, then there is no law, no rightful government, and chaos and anarchy reign. If the human race does not have the power to take the life of any killer of human life, then mankind does not have dominion over all the earth.[3]

It is perfectly clear that the movement for so-called "abolition of capital punishment" is not aimed at the power of the state to kill, but rather at the exercise of punishment. At least one of the proponents of the bill before the Texas Legislature to abolish capital punishment has admitted the point and written that he does not oppose the power of the state to kill in cases of riot, insurrection or rebellion. Others stated before the committee of the House in Austin at its hearing on the bill in 1961 that they had no opposition to the power of the state to kill in war.

Perhaps one of the most striking illustrations of what is at stake really is in the State of Israel, a showcase of socialism, which has abolished capital punishment. That government, as manifest in the Eichmann case, has by no means given up the power to take human life; it has merely set up a purportedly whole new basis for conditions upon which it deems itself proper in carrying out the sentence of death. What it has abolished is not the "death" in "death penalty," but the penalty normally prescribed in civilized society. What is under attack by the abolitionists is not simply the chief punishment, but all punishment as now recognized in the Christian world. What Dr. Silber really is fulminating against is not killing, but punishment for moral crimes based upon the Ten Commandments which is the legal system of the United States and all Christian nations. In fact, what is abolished under the abolitionist schemes is the whole concept of retributive justice, the only justice that can be administered by the state.

Curiously enough, that fact is never mentioned. It is never so much as whispered that the purpose of criminal law is, first of all, the "punishment of crime." It is well to bear in mind that the Texas Legal Code includes some novelties in its preamble by adding that penalties are also to reform the offender and deter crime. The abolitionists never come to grips with the profound problem of justice and punishment, but rave wildly about the questionable subsidiary purpose of deterrence of acts of violence.

The chosen battleground is plainly a diversionary effort to direct attention away from the real peril: nobody could ever establish whether or not any law has satisfactorily been a "deterrent to crime." The factors involved in the commission of crime are so manifold, so diverse and so inscrutable that it is impossible to determine what has hindered the commission of one more. To be sure, we humans would be confident that the administration of justice is a deterrent to crime: but that is an article of pure faith and no more. It is not subject to demonstration or proof. We simply believe in law and its administration by due authority. To slip from the question of whether the state may legally and properly administer justice to the proposition that those who believe it may must "be able to show that it is indispensable for the protection and preservation of other lives" is a non-sequitur and an absurdity. Since when did the State of Texas have to show any such thing in order to carry out, under due process, the punishment of death or any other punishment? It does these things in order to uphold the law. It is really the law itself that is challenged here.

That Dr. Silber agrees with the real issue is to be seen from the quotation he uses from Dr. Sheldon Glueck, of Harvard, that "The presence of the death penalty as the keynote of our penal system bedevils the administration of criminal justice all the way down the line and *is the stumbling block in the path of general reform in the treatment of crime and criminals*" (italics mine). Both the objective of the abolitionists and a recognition of the chief obstacle in their way are here set forth. The objective is "general reform in the treatment of crime and criminals." What stands in the way is admittedly "the keystone of our penal system." Notice it is not a reform or tightening up of the administration that is sought, not a purifying of the judges and a cleansing of the prosecutors, but a complete overhauling of the system, beginning at its keystone. Even Hitler and Khrushchev have not been more plain or precise in their declared purpose to "bury you."

These abolitionists refuse to discuss our penal system. It is too deep and imbedded in what is "us." To perform a general reform in the treatment of crime and criminals, beginning at the keystone, is to seek a general reform of the whole body politic —that is, a smashing of the "status quo" (created order) and a vainly imagined substitution of a re-shaped or restructured one. Even if we were to allow, as I certainly do not, that our penal system is like a raging cancer, the proposed surgery would not only remove the cancer but also the life of the victim. It is, therefore, much more to their purpose simply to perform the surgery while staging a sham demonstration of controversy over the question of how many crimes have been forestalled by the administration of justice. They do not tell us they want to demolish the whole Biblical concept of retributive justice, upon which rests the work of Christ in atoning for the sins of the world; and to eradicate the state as the "minister of God to execute wrath,"[4] and to destroy the whole system of Christian law based upon, derived from and limited by the Ten Commandments (cf. Blackstone). Even allowing the preposterous claim that these revolutionists could conceivably build a new social order on better principles, it is a perilous venture to let them do first the necessary work of wiping the slate clean—that is, of destroying us—in order to raise a new structure on the ashes.

Nobody would quarrel with the abhorrence of death: the modern abolitionists have no monopoly on the milk of human sympathy or kindness or delicacy. However, it does not follow that death inflicted by a murderer is less to be abhorred than death inflicted by due process upon the murderer as a just retribution for his crime. Life imprisonment, Dr. Silber notwithstanding, is by no means "the alternative" to the death penalty. Neither is it more merciful, nor, as has been sometimes declared, more cruel. It is simply one of a thousand conceivable "lesser penalties" whose infliction all depend upon the power of the state to inflict the chief one.

Christian people have never for a moment supposed that life is totally ruled by the state, and that all power is subsumed in the power to kill. Most of our public life is regulated by the power of Christ to make alive and to forgive, and no discussion of our penal system is complete without an analysis of the Christian economy of two powers and the Church's independent power to administer penitence, forgiveness and instruction.

Christian governments are rather carefully regulated in their rights and duties to punish wickedness and vice by administration of laws derived from the Ten Commandments: but no concept of Christianity can be abolished. Only the modern revolutionaries, who are dedicated to a new world order, can so defy God as to seek to reform all that has been wrought by Him and to construct a new system on entirely new principles, beginning at the head corner stone. It is quite true that the keystone of the present, Christian, penal system is the death penalty. When that is taken away, so is the natural sovereignty of the State of Texas, and the whole civilized order structured upon Biblical revelation and control. The death penalty is the crucial point at which it is determined whether or not this people shall continue to be a people under God, or whether we shall repudiate God's system of criminal justice and fall at the feet of human constructs of society in terms of a new order which knows no power but that of the prince of this world.

Footnotes:

(1) John Locke, "Of Civil Government" Book II, Ch. 1, 3; (2) John 18:36; (3) Gen. 1:26, 9:1ff, et al; (4) Romans 13.4.

V

Is Capital Punishment Wrong?

by

JACOB J. VELLENGA

The Church at large is giving serious thought to capital punishment. Church councils and denominational assemblies are making strong pronouncements against it. We are hearing such arguments as: "Capital punishment brutalizes society by cheapening life." "Capital punishment is morally indefensible." "Capital punishment is no deterrent to murder." "Capital punishment makes it impossible to rehabilitate the criminal."

But many of us are convinced that the Church should not meddle with capital punishment. Church members should be strong in supporting good legislation, militant against wrong laws, opposed to weak and partial law enforcement. But we should be sure that what we endorse or what we oppose is intimately related to the common good, the benefit of society, the establishment of justice, and the upholding of high moral and ethical standards.

There is a good reason for saying that opposition to capital punishment is not for the common good but sides with evil; shows more regard for the criminal than the victim of the crime; weakens justice and encourages murder; is not based on Scripture but on a vague philosophical system that makes a fetish of the idea that the taking of life is wrong, under every circumstance, and fails to distinguish adequately between killing and murder, between punishment and crime.

Capital punishment is a controversial issue upon which good people are divided, both sides having high motives in their respective convictions. But capital punishment should not be classified with social evils like segregation, racketeering, liquor traffic, and gambling.

These evils are clearly antisocial, while capital punishment is a matter of jurisprudence established for the common good and benefit of society. Those favoring capital punishment are not to be stigmatized as heartless, vengeful, and lacking in mercy, but are to be respected as advocating that which is the best for society as a whole. When we stand for the common good, we must of necessity be strongly opposed to that behavior which is contrary to the common good.

From time immemorial the conviction of good society has been that life is sacred, and he who violates the sacredness of life through murder must pay the supreme penalty. This ancient belief is well expressed in Scripture: "Only you shall not eat flesh with its life, that is, its blood. For your lifeblood I will surely require a reckoning; of every beast I will require it and of man; of every man's brother

I will require the life of man. Whoever sheds the blood of man, by man shall his blood be shed; for God made man in his own image" (Gen. 9:4-6, RSV). Life is sacred. He who violates the law must pay the supreme penalty, just because life is sacred. Life is sacred since God made man in His image. There is a distinction here between murder and penalty.

Many who oppose capital punishment make a strong argument out of the Sixth Commandment: "Thou shalt not kill" (Exod. 20:13). But they fail to note the commentary on that Commandment which follows: "Whoever strikes a man so that he dies shall be put to death . . . If a man wilfully attacks another to kill him treacherously, you shall take him from my altar that he may die" (Exod. 21:12, 14). It is faulty exegesis to take a verse of Scripture out of its context and interpret it without regard to its qualifying words.

The Exodus reference is not the only one referring to capital punishment. In Leviticus 24:17 we read: "He who kills a man shall be put to death." Numbers 35:30-34 goes into more detail on the subject: "If any one kills a person, the murderer shall be put to death on the evidence of witnesses; but no person shall be put to death on the testimony of one witness. Moreover you shall accept no ransom for the life of a murderer who is guilty of death; but he shall be put to death . . . You shall not thus pollute the land in which you live; for blood pollutes the land, and no expiation can be made for the land, for the blood that is shed in it, except by the blood of him who shed it. You shall not defile the land in which you live, in the midst of which I dwell; for I the Lord dwell in the midst of the people of Israel." (Compare Deut. 17:6-7 and 19:11-13.)

Deuteronomy 19:4-6, 10 distinguishes between accidental killing and wilful murder: "If any one kills his neighbor unintentionally without having been at enmity with him in time past . . . he may flee to one of these cities (cities of refuge) and save his life; lest the avenger of blood in hot anger pursue the manslayer and overtake him, because the way is long, and wound him mortally, though the man did not deserve to die, since he was not at enmity with his neighbor in time past . . . lest innocent blood be shed in your land which the Lord your God gives you for an inheritance, and so the guilt of bloodshed be upon you."

The cry of the prophets against social evils was not only directed against discrimination of the poor, and the oppression of widows and orphans, but primarily against laxness in the administration of justice. They were opposed to the laws being flouted and criminals not being punished. A vivid expression of the prophet's attitude is recorded in Isaiah: "Justice is turned back, and righteousness stands afar off; for truth has fallen in the public squares, and uprightness cannot enter . . . The Lord saw it and it displeased him that there was no justice. He saw that there was no man, and wondered that there was no one to intervene; then his own arm brought him victory, and his righteousness upheld him. He put on righteousness as a breastplate, and a helmet of salvation upon his head; he put on garments of vengeance for clothing and wrapped himself in a fury as a mantle. According to their deeds, so will he repay, wrath to his adversaries, requital to his enemies." (Isa. 59:14-18).

The teachings of the New Testament are in harmony with the Old Testament. Christ came to fulfill the law, not to destroy the basic principles of law and order, righteousness and justice. In Matthew 5:17-20 we read: "Think not that I have come to abolish the law and the prophets: I have come not to abolish them but to fulfill them. For truly, I say to you, till heaven and earth pass away, not an iota, not a dot, will pass from the law until all is accomplished . . . For I tell you, unless your righteousness exceeds that of the scribes and Pharisees, you will never enter the kingdom of heaven."

Then Christ speaks of hate and murder: "You have heard that it was said to the men of old, 'You shall not kill; and whoever kills shall be liable to judgment (capital punishment).' But I say to you that everyone who is angry with his brother shall be liable to judgment (capital punishment)" (Matt. 5:21-22). It is evident that Jesus was not condemning the established law of capital punishment, but was actually saying that hate deserved capital punishment. Jesus was not advocating doing away with capital punishment but urging his followers to live above the law so that law and punishment could not touch them. To live above the law is not the same as abrogating it.

The Church, the Body of Christ, has enough to do

to evangelize and educate society to live above the law and positively to influence society to high and noble living by maintaining a wide margin between right and wrong. The early Christians did not meddle with laws against wrong doing. Paul expresses this attitude in his letter to the Romans: "Therefore, he who resists the authorities resists what God has appointed, and those who resist will incur judgment. For rulers are not a terror to good conduct, but to bad . . . for he is God's servant for your good. But if you do wrong, be afraid, for he does not bear the sword in vain; he is the servant of God to execute his wrath on the wrongdoer" (13:2-4).

The early Christians suffered many injustices and were victims of inhuman treatment. Many became martyrs because of their faith. Consequently, they were often tempted to take the law in their own hands. But Paul cautioned them: "Beloved, never avenge yourselves, but leave it to the wrath of God; for it is written, 'Vengeance is mine, I will repay, says the Lord.' No, 'if your enemy is hungry, feed him; if he is thirsty, give him drink; for by so doing you will heap burning coals upon his head' " (Rom. 12:19-21).

There is not a hint of indication in the New Testament that laws should be changed to make it lenient for the wrongdoer. Rather the whole trend is that the Church leave matters of justice and law enforcement to the government in power. "Let every person be subject to the governing authorities. For there is no authority except from God, and those that exist have been instituted by God" (Rom. 13:1).

Note the juxtaposition of love to enemies with a healthy respect for government. The Christian fellowship is not to take law in its own hands, for God has government in his economy in order to take care of matters of justice.

Jesus' words on loving one's enemies, turning the other cheek, and walking the second mile were not propaganda to change jurisprudence, but they were meant to establish a new society not merely made up of law-abiding citizens but those who lived a life higher than the law, so that stealing, adultery, and murder would become inoperative, but not annulled. The law of love, also called the law of liberty, was not presented to do away with the natural laws of society, but to inaugurate a new concept of law written on the heart where the mainsprings of action are born. The Church is ever to strive for superior law and order, not to advocate a lower order that makes wrongdoing less culpable.

Love and mercy have no stability without agreement on basic justice and fair play. Mercy always infers a tacit recognition that justice and rightness are to be expected. Lowering the standards of justice is never to be a substitute for the concept of mercy. The Holy God does not show mercy contrary to his righteousness but in harmony with it. This is why the awful Cross was necessary and a righteous Christ had to hang on it. This is why God's redemption is always conditioned by one's heart attitude. There is no forgiveness for anyone who is unforgiving. "Forgive us our debts, as we forgive our debtors" (Matt. 6:12). There is no mercy for anyone who will not be merciful. "Blessed are the merciful for they shall obtain mercy" (Matt. 5:7). There is striking similarity to these verses in Psalm 18:25-26: "With the loyal thou dost show thyself loyal; with the blameless man thou dost show thyself blameless; with the pure thou dost show thyself pure; and with the crooked thou dost show thyself perverse."

Professor C. S. Lewis in his recent book *Reflections on the Psalms* deals with the difficult subject of the spirit of hatred which is in some of the Psalms. He points out that these hatreds had a good motivation. "Such hatreds are the kind of thing that cruelty and injustice, by a sort of natural law, produce . . . Not to perceive it at all—not even to be tempted to resentment—to accept it as the most ordinary thing in the world—argues a terrifying insensibility. Thus the absence of anger, especially that sort of anger which we call indignation, can, in my opinion, be a most alarming symptom . . . If the Jews cursed more bitterly than the Pagans this was, I think, at least in part because they took right and wrong more seriously."

Vindictiveness is a sin, but only because a sense of justice has gotten out of hand. The check on revenge must be in the careful and exact administering of justice by society's government. This is the clear teaching of Scripture in both the Old and New Testaments. The Church and individual Christians should be active in their witness to the Gospel of love and forgiveness and ever lead people to the high law of love of God and our neighbors as ourselves; but meanwhile wherever and whenever God's love and mercy are rejected, as in crime, natural law and order must prevail, not as extraneous to redemption but as part of the whole scope of God's dealings with man.

The argument that capital punishment rules out the possibility of repentance for crime is unrealistic. If a wanton killer does not repent when the sentence of death is upon him, he certainly will not repent if he has 20 to 50 years of life imprisonment ahead of him.

We, who are supposed to be Christian, make too much of physical life. Jesus said, "And do not fear those who kill the body but cannot kill the soul; rather fear him who can destroy both soul and body in hell" (Matt. 10:28). Laxness in law tends to send both soul and body to hell. It is more than a pious remark when a judge says to the condemned criminal: "And may God have mercy on your soul." The sentence of death on a killer is more redemptive than the tendency to excuse his crime as no worse than grand larceny.

It is significant that when Jesus voluntarily went the way of the Cross he chose the capital punishment of His day as His instrument to save the world. And when He gave redemption to the repentant thief He did not save him from capital punishment but gave him Paradise instead which was far better. We see again that mercy and forgiveness are something different from being excused from wrongdoing.

No one can deny that the execution of a murderer is a horrible spectacle. But we must not forget that murder is more horrible. The supreme penalty should be exacted only after the guilt is established beyond the shadow of a doubt and only for wanton, willful, premeditated murder. But the law of capital punishment must stand, no matter how often a jury recommends mercy. The law of capital punishment must stand as a silent but powerful witness to the sacredness of God-given life. Words are not enough to show that life is sacred. Active justice must be administered when the sacredness of life is violated.

It is recognized that this article will only impress those who are convinced that the Scriptures of the Old and New Testament are the supreme authority of faith and practice. If one accepts the authority of Scripture, then the issue of capital punishment must be decided on what Scripture actually teaches and not on the popular, naturalistic ideas of sociology and penology that prevail today. One generation's thinking is not enough to comprehend the implications of the age-old problem of murder. We need the best thinking of the ages on how best to deal with crime and punishment. We need the Word of God to guide us.

VI

The Scripture and Capital Punishment

by

W. A. BARNETT

There is a widespread belief that Christian teachings oppose capital punishment. Many Christians who regard capital punishment as necessary for a well ordered society reason indirectly that since crime is evil, and capital punishment is a deterrent to crime, and since Christian teachings embrace a well ordered society, it therefore may be conjectured that capital punishment is Christian in principle. But many Christians who favor capital punishment seriously doubt that it has any support in Christian Scripture.

Yet if Christian teachings be lacking in doctrines that pertain to capital punishment, then Christian teachings do not constitute a complete, comprehensive social ideology. For any such ideology will certainly include provisions for the punishment of criminals. If Christian teaching be thus defective in providing the solution to major social and political problems, Christian teaching must then recognize some other ideology as having a superior capacity in an era in which it has an inadequate capacity.

But if Christian teaching lays claim to being a complete social ideology, there must be somewhere in the Source of Christian teaching passages which support the principle of criminal punishment.

We must consider whether our neglect of such passages has caused us to limit the application of Christian precepts to the merely personal aspects of life to the exclusion of any Christian purpose that may be found in Scripture for humanity as a whole. For, if Christian teachings do not embrace a social concept comprehensive enough to include criminal punishment, then the Christian religion belongs to the same category as Yogi, Mesmerism, Christian Science, Self-Realization, Voodoo and Gnosticism. A careful study of such spiritual religions reveals their lack of social and political concepts.

On the other hand, however, if Christian teachings apply to social and political problems at all, to what *extent* do they *apply?* To ask the same question another way, at what point do Christian principles stop and secular principles take over?

To bring the issue down to earth, can a policeman be a Christian? Or, can a Christian do the work of a policeman? If we adopt the reasoning that no Christian should try to affect the behavior of another human being by force, then Christian teachings are incompatible with an orderly society. If, on the other hand, it is possible for a policeman to make an arrest by use of force or threat of force and remain true to Christian teachings, then Christianity is compatible with an orderly society.

On another score, if after arrest, indictment, and

conviction, the death sentence is denied as being inconsistent with the Christian concept of justice, is it consistent with Christian justice to impose upon an innocent society the burden of ever-expanding prison costs?

But, if Christian teachings embrace the death penalty, do they not also embrace the responsibility of Christians to demand that sentences be based on justice? If Christians refrain from participating in judicial processes and punishment is meted out unjustly by some secular court, would not this blood be upon the hands of those Christians who withdrew their Christian influence from the political realm? Those who would keep Christ out of government, would keep Him out of the courts, and purposely and with intent would encourage atheists to rule the courts of justice.

Before turning our attention to the passages which have a direct bearing on capital punishment, let us first consider what would have happened if the Good Samaritan, of Luke 10:25-36, had arrived in time to have witnessed the robbing and beating of the victim to whom he gave comfort. Would he have been justified in using violence to protect the victim, if necessary? If he had needed to use extreme measures, would our Lord still have considered the story a lesson in charity? In other words is ours a religion that is effective only so long as it does not encounter violence?

Some of the passages from the New Testament which support the administration of capital punishment, compatible to the Christian faith, are as follows:

Luke 19:27—"But those mine enemies, which would not that I should reign over them, bring hither and slay them before me."

Luke 22:36—" . . . and he (of the number of Christians) that hath no sword, let him sell his cloak and buy one."

Acts 3:23—". . . every soul, which will not hear that Prophet, shall be destroyed from among the people."

Romans 1:32—". . . they which commit such things are worthy of death . . ."

II Thess. 1:6—". . . a righteous thing with God to recompense tribulation to them that trouble you."

The above passages are representative of a larger number which support capital punishment, but which more conspicuously presuppose Christian control of the machinery of the civil state.

Another group of passages, often used to enjoin Christian loyalty to anti-Christian regimes are as follows:

Acts 25:11—". . . For if I be an offender, or have committed anything worthy of death I refuse not to die . . ."

Rom. 13:4—"For he (the Roman magistrate) is the minister of God to thee for good. But if thou do that which is evil, be afraid; for he beareth not the sword in vain . . ."

Titus 3:1—"Put them in mind to be subject to principalities, and powers, to obey magistrates, to be ready to every good work . . ."

I Peter 2:13-14—"Submit yourselves to every ordinance of man for the Lord's sake; whether it be to the king as supreme; Or to governors, as unto them that are sent by him for the punishment of evil doers, and for the praise of them that do well."

Each of the above passages enjoined Christians to obey the laws of the Roman Empire during the reign of Claudius, and the first part of the reign of Nero. Yet there is no reason to suppose that the references enjoin Christians to obey any anti-Christian laws or the decrees of any anti-Christian tyrant of any century. It would be absurd to interpret the New Testament as enjoining Christians to submit to laws which contradict Christian teachings.

The Apostle Paul did not write of the Roman government as a hostile government but a paternal government. As Dr. Marcus Dods wrote in his discussion of the Epistles to the Thessalonians:

But the actual circumstances in which Paul was placed, as described in the Book of Acts, give us the key to the true interpretation of the passage. The Jews were the chief danger of the infant Church. It was by the Jews the Apostle himself had everywhere been opposed and maltreated; and it was by them also the Thessalonians were now being persecuted. But again and again in Paul's experience the Jewish hostility was thwarted by the Roman magistracy, and wherever he went it became more evident that but for the protection accorded to him and his converts by the imperial justice and authority, the Christian Church would be crushed.

The severity of modern anti-Christian tyranny, coupled with the impression that the Roman government of New Testament times was anti-Christian in principle, has led many to place the Rome of Claudius in the same category with the Russia of Stalin. There came a time when Christians were hounded throughout the Roman Empire, but the persecution was almost invariably more personal than it was official. Although the government of Rome was never pro-Christian in any positive sense, the Church at the beginning enjoyed an official benevolence and thrived under official protection.

For instance: the story of the trial of Jesus suggests that while His enemies secured His condemnation and death, their enmity was not derived from the law of Rome or from the official attitude of Rome (Matt. 27:19). It was Rome which rescued Paul from the Jewish mob (Acts 21:31-32), protected him from ambush (Acts 22:23ff), delivered him from an unjust sentence (Acts 25:11-12).

There was, therefore, no reason why the Christian Church should not have assumed that loyalty to sympathetic civil authority and approval of the power wielded by such civil authority, was of the faith.

The Creeds of the Church have traditionally upheld this view. The Westminster Confession is clear (Chapter XXV) and other confessions agree. For instance, Sections 1 and 2 of Article XXIV of the Philadelphia Confession, otherwise known as the Old London Confession of the Baptists of 1689 reads:

"1. God, the supreme Lord, and King of all the world, hath ordained civil magistrates to be under

Him, over the people, for His own glory and the public good; and to this end hath armed them with the power of the sword, for defence and encouragement of them that do good, and for the punishment of evil doers.

"2. It is lawful for Christians to accept and execute the office of a magistrate, when called thereunto; in the management whereof, as they ought especially to maintain justice and peace, according to the wholesome laws of each kingdom, and commonwealth; so for that end they may lawfully now under the New Testament wage war, upon just and necessary occasions."

VII

Medicine or Morals as the Basis of Justice and Law

E. L. H. TAYLOR

According to an old Greek legend, a wooden horse was once constructed by Epeus to enable the Greeks to capture the city of Troy. After trying unsuccessfully for ten years to capture the city by force, the Greeks turned to a clever stratagem. They pretended to sail away back to Greece, and left a huge wooden horse filled with armed men. While the Trojans were examining the horse, Sinon, a Greek, put in an appearance and was captured posing as the victim of Odysseus' hatred. He told them that the horse was an offering to the goddess Athena, and that it would bring disaster to the Greeks if taken into the city. When Laocoon, a priest of Poseidon, advised the Trojans against dragging the horse inside the walls of Troy, two huge snakes appeared and overpowered both Laocoon and his two sons. The Trojans were convinced, both by Sinon's lies and by the prodigy of the snakes, and pulled the wooden horse into the city with songs and festivity. That night Sinon let out the armed Greek soldiers enclosed within the horse's huge wooden body, the gates of the city were opened to the rest of the Greek forces who had returned to the beaches during the night, and the mighty city of Troy was captured, burned and destroyed. King Priam was slain and King Menelaus regained possession of Helen.

By a similar stratagem pyschiatrists and penologists are seeking to undermine our historic system of Christian law and justice in all English-speaking lands using as their "Trojan Horse" current theories of "mental health" and of "social and legal engineering." Upon achieving independence the founding fathers of the United States rightly adopted the best elements in the former British tradition of government and the Rule of Law under which the Thirteen Colonies previously had been governed. According to this tradition which can be traced back to the Biblical conception of human nature as created in God's holy image, each of us from the President and the Queen down to the humblest village policeman is held responsible to God's higher Moral Law. In his classic work THE LAW OF THE CONSTITUTION the late Professor A. V. Dicey of Oxford University refers to this doctrine of individual responsibility as one of the two principles which underlie the whole law of the British Constitution, and the maintenance of which has gone a long way both to ensure the supremacy of The Rule of Law and ultimately to curb the arbitrariness of the Executive branch of British States. "The first of these principles," he writes, "is that every wrong doer is individually responsible for every unlawful act in which he takes part . . . and cannot plead in his defense that he did it under the orders of a master or superior. This doctrine of individual responsibility is the real foundation of the legal dogma that the orders of the King (and we may add the President) are no justification for the commission of a wrongful or illegal act. The ordinary rule therefore that every wrong doer is individually responsible and liable for the wrong he has committed is the foundation on which rests the great constitutional doctrine of Ministerial responsibility."[1]

Dicey then points out that the second principle underlying the British Constitution is that the Courts give a remedy for the infringement of a right whether the injury done be great or small. The Common Law of America as of England protects our right to personal liberty against every kind of infringement, and gives the same redress for the pettiest as for the gravest invasions of personal freedom. "Few features in our legal system," Dicey writes, "have done more to maintain the authority of the Law than the fact that all offences great and small are dealt with on the same principles and by the same courts. The Common Law of England (and of America, we may add) today knows nothing of exceptional offences punished by extraordinary tribunals."[2]

Our British and American Common Law not only punishes every kind of unlawful interference with a man's personal freedom, but also provides adequate security that everyone who is imprisoned without legal justification shall be able to obtain his freedom. This security is provided by the celebrated writ of "habeas corpus" and of the Habeas Corpus Acts.

In the Great Charter of Liberty which was exacted from King John in 1215, there was a provision that "no free man shall be taken or imprisoned, or evicted from his land, or outlawed or exiled, or in any way harassed; nor will we go up on him nor will we send upon him save by the lawful judgment of his peers, or by the law of the land." King John made this promise but it was not always kept because there was no court procedure by which a freeman could secure his release from prison when sent there by the king's orders. Not until the reign of Charles II in 1679 was the right of the citizen made effective by the passage of the Habeas Corpus Act. This act permitted anyone who felt himself unjustly detained to sue out a writ before the courts. A writ of habeas corpus is an order issued by the Courts of the Realm, calling upon a person by whom a prisoner is alleged to be kept in confinement to bring such a prisoner—"to have his body," whence the name, before the Courts to let the Courts know on what ground the prisoner is confined and so to give the Courts the opportunity of dealing with the prisoner as the law may require. The essence of the whole transaction is that the Court can by writ of habeas corpus cause any citizen who is wrongfully imprisoned by the Government of the United States or of the United Kingdom Government to be actually brought before the Court and thus find out why he is imprisoned, and then having him before the Court, either then and there release him or else see that he is dealt with in whatever way the law requires and that he be brought speedily to a proper trial.

The privilege of the writ of habeas corpus has become in England and America one of the great safeguards against the abuse of power. Unfortunately, however, the British authorities developed the practice of persuading Parliament to pass special acts temporarily suspending the privilege of the writ. The framers of the American Constitution were afraid that Congress might fall into the same habit, hence they inserted the provision that "The privilege of the writ of habeas corpus shall not be suspended, unless when in cases of rebellion or invasion the public safety may require it."[3]

As a result of this wonderful privilege enjoyed by every citizen of America and Britain we can all sleep in our beds at night knowing that we shall not be arrested by any secret police as has happened to so many innocent persons in Nazi Germany and Communist lands during our century. We are apt to consider the writ of habeas corpus in terms of the rights of the individual, but a right presupposes a value. According to the Common Law each individual citizen must be treated with proper respect, even with a kind of reverence. Our Common Law does not explicitly assert that man is a child of God, but where systems of law have arisen, as in Nazi Germany and Communist Russia, which explicitly deny that man is a child of God, there is no writ of habeas corpus and those who are displeasing to the authorities simply disappear into the darkness of the night leaving no trace of their whereabouts. It is a moot question how long the writ of habeas corpus would be available in Great Britain or in the United States of America if a different doctrine of man were to prevail, a scientific humanist doctrine of man for example, such as today lies behind most current sociology, penology, and criminal psychology.[4]

Of all the sinister movements which have plagued us during our century, none bodes more evil for our future well being as FREE men and women than the present campaign now being waged throughout the English-speaking world to place our historic legal system upon this so-called "scientific" doctrine of man and the attempt to substitute medicine for morals as the yardstick of American and British Justice. Under cover of the honourable profession of medicine, arrogant "social scientists," "penologists" and psychiatrists are seeking to subvert our most cherished legal, political and moral values.

Whereas a hundred years ago the expert in mental medicine claimed to be able to deal only with violent or deluded patients, or with those who were unmanageably hysterical, depressed to the point of total incapacity, or senile to the point of infantilism; today the psychiatrist arrogantly demands the LEGAL right to treat and to "brainwash" the whole population. Children who steal or have violent tempers or who wet their beds, men and women who cannot get on with their spouses, business trainees and service personnel, and above all vicious criminals convicted of the most brutal crimes—all these are today to be referred to the psychiatric doctor. Thanks to their insidious propaganda by press, radio and television millions of people who a generation ago would have had the honesty to admit that they were sinful, disobedient, unfaithful or wicked, as the case might be, now claim, of course, the reason that they behaved as badly as they did is because they are "sick" and in need of treatment by medical rather than moral or perhaps penal methods.

Superficially considered, this change of attitude is acclaimed on all sides as a step in the direction of progress. Actually, it can only be explained as the expression of the steady encroachment by medical science upon territory till lately occupied by Christian morality and the Christian life and world-view. Instead of repenting of his sins as his grandfather did, modern man now thinks he can redeem himself and his fellow men by the application of scientific method to his personal and social life. In some respects this new struggle between the rival empires of apostate humanistic social science and Christian morality based upon the Holy Scriptures, seems to be the contemporary equivalent of the Nineteenth Century battle between biological and Biblical explanations of man's nature, origin and destiny. True the modern battle is much more politely conducted than was that which agitated our Victorian grandparents. So decorous, indeed, is it that it is not recognized by Christians in the English speaking world as being a battle at all. But the issues are akin and the consequences will be just as serious. Thus, psychiatrists and "social scientists" since Freud and Pavlov have been busy doing for man's morals, politics and laws what Charles Darwin and Thomas Huxley tried to do for his pedigree. For Dr. Edward Glover, co-founder of the Institute for the Study and Treatment of Delinquency, all this is a matter of rejoicing in the secular humanist heart. "When the social historian of the future looks back to the first half of the 20th Century," he writes in his book THE ROOTS OF CRIME, "it will by then be apparent that amongst the revolutionary changes to be credited to that period, two at least were of vital importance to the development of humanism; the liberation of psychology from the fetters of a conscious rationalism; and the subsequent emancipation of sociology from the more primitive superstitions and moralistic conceptions of crime."[5]

Dr. Glover then blithely dismisses such uniquely human reactions as having a guilty conscience after wrong doing as merely the expression of unconscious fixations imposed by the human ape's so-called "Super-Ego" upon his animal "Ego." Instead of man having been created in God's holy image and endowed with a sense of responsibility to God for his actions, he is really only the product of his animal heredity acting upon his physical and social environment.

In terms of this new so-called "scientific" doctrine of man criminals cannot possibly be held responsible for their misdeeds because they are psychologically sick rather than morally sinful. No one holds us responsible for the silly things that we may say or do in the delirium of a high fever. By the same logic, once it is admitted that the human mind can be sick as well as the body, we must expect those who suffer from mental illness of whatever degree to make the same claim to be relieved of personal responsibility for their actions as do those persons whose incapacity is obviously due to purely physical symptoms. From all sides we are being asked to assimilate mental and physical illness. In a report accepted in 1961 by the General Council of the United Church of Canada (Methodists and Presbyterians) the Federal Government of Canada was urged to send ALL convicted criminals, including murderers, to hospitals and clinics rather than to prisons.[6]

As a result of all this psychological double-talk, the rest of us orthodox Christians are being asked to bring in a completely new legal system based UPON MEDICAL AND NON-CHRISTIAN AND FREUDIAN DOCTRINES ABOUT MAN, RATHER THAN UPON THE BIBLICAL DOCTRINE OF MAN AS CREATED IN GOD'S IMAGE AND AS A SINNER. After all, doctors as doctors are trained to deal with people who are in some sense sick; and the fact that the naughty child, the unhappy lover, and the law-breaker now pass through the doctor's consulting rooms implies the belief that people in these predicaments are sick rather than sinful. Thus the medical concept of illness has been rapidly expanding at the expense of the Biblical concept of sin and moral failure. Illness, of course must be treated by medical science—unlike moral failure, for which personal effort and repentance on the part of the sinner himself, perhaps accompanied by exhortation, or punishment administered by parent, teacher, magistrate or friend, are appropriate. And so science having supposedly defeated the Word of God over the riddles of the Universe, now seeks to usurp the role of Christian morality derived from Biblical revelation in deciding how we should conduct our lives, organize our legal system and "treat" our socially maladjusted citizens.

Let all concerned Christians take note. Such a substitution of medicine for morals as the yardstick of our present system of Christian law and justice will involve nothing less than a fundamental revolution in the existing conception and structure of Christian law paving the way for the totalitarian enslavement of the WHOLE population by the social conditioners and planners; an enslavement so graphically portrayed by George Orwell's horror story of the future, NINETEEN EIGHTY-FOUR. Thus does God punish those who overthrow the Moral Order of His Universe. Up till now the main function of the Law Courts in the English-speaking world has been to determine whether or not persons accused of crime committed the ACT in question. Such psychological considerations as motive are taken into account only when they have a bearing on the probability or improbability of guilt, or in murder cases where insanity can be pleaded. Our Christian legal system is based on the Biblical assumptions:

(1) That everybody, except children and lunatics, knows the difference between right and wrong. Thanks to the operations of God's Temporal Conserving or Common Grace upon our consciences we still can tell the difference between acts of right and acts of wrong doing.

(2) That everybody apart from children and lunatics is able to choose between doing right and doing wrong. In other words in spite of original sin man still retains a relative measure of moral freedom. The cannibal can choose whether or not he will eat his wife or his uncle! According to the Lord Jesus Christ man is NOT merely the product of his heredity acting upon his environment. Man's personality or "heart" is the product of the response he makes to his Creator as well as to his heredity and environment. And the kind of response he makes depends partly upon himself. Allow me to quote some words of Christ Himself:—

"Listen to me . . . nothing that goes into a man from the OUTSIDE can defile him; no, it is the things that come out of him that defile a man . . . nothing that goes from outside into a man can defile him because it does not enter into his heart but into his stomach and so passes down the drain. For from inside, OUT OF A MAN'S HEART come evil thoughts, acts of fornicating, of theft, murder, adultery, ruthless greed, and malice, fraud, indecency, envy, slander, arrogance and folly; these evil things all come from the inside and they defile the man." (New English Bible. St. Mark 7:14-23.)

Out of the human heart are the issues of life. The human heart is the concentration point, the religious root of our entire human existence. Out of it arise all our deeds, thoughts, feelings and desires. In our heart we give answer to the most profound and ultimate questions, and in our heart our relationship to God is determined. The heart or soul of man may never be identified with any of our vital functions such as feeling or thinking or doing. It is deeper than any vital function and it transcends the temporal. It is not possible to give a scientific conceptual definition of the heart, because as the centre of our whole existence, the heart is the deepest created presupposition of our thinking. Christians can only repeat through their faith what God has revealed to them in His Word concerning this central reality of our lives.[7]

Of course no Christian wishes to deny the hindrances to man's freedom caused by both original and personal sinfulness and by centuries of accumulated social sin; but the power of these influences to prevent freedom of choice is found only amongst the insane. It is upon this issue that orthodox Christians are bound to take issue with modern social scientists. Today psychiatrists and sociologists have for too long been absorbed with the condition of the abnormal and sub-normal. The result is that they are forever looking for evidences of the abnormal in us all, and where they do not find it they invent it. Modern social scientists seem bent on spending their time in a vain attempt to convince men, women and juveniles that they cannot help doing what they do, that they are in the power of sex-urges, repressions, mother-fixations, and a whole host of other unconscious neuroses, inhibitions and psychoses.

(3) A third Christian principle underlying our legal system is that anyone who chooses to do wrong should be properly punished for it and that the State must only punish men for the *crimes* they commit,

not for all sins for which they are guilty. In other words Christians believe that punishment is the price we pay for our freedom to choose evil deeds in preference to good deeds.

God's Holy Spirit acting upon a man's darkened conscience tells him that he ought to do this and ought NOT to do that. This would be nonsense unless he were relatively free to do this and not to do that. For the same reason because it is his choice to do this and not to do that, he must be held responsible for doing this and not doing the other. This Christian emphasis upon personal responsibility has become greatly blurred in recent years. A whole profession has grown up whose sole service to society consists in offering ready-made excuses for human conduct, however base and bestial that conduct may be. Our Courts of Justice are rapidly becoming platforms where medico-legal experts display their expertise in excusing criminals for their vicious conduct and where any accused, no matter how ghastly the crime he is being tried for, can mitigate his punishment by claiming that "he saw something nasty in the woodshed when he was a young child."

(4) Another Christian assumption upon which our legal system has been based is what is called the principle of retributive justice. Briefly stated this declares that no one should be punished unless in actual fact he has committed some definite crime. Punishment is necessarily tied to wrong doing and guilt. It can only be justified as the expiation and atonement and satisfaction for guilt. Thus guilt is

a necessary condition of punishment. Strictly speaking you cannot be punished for something you have not done wrong, though you may be made to suffer for it. Philosophers and theologians have often discussed how far punishment is a deterrent, how far it is disciplinary or reformative, and whether it should ever be retributive in character. On this question I can only say that punishment is not defensible morally speaking as a deterrent, and it is not likely to be remedial or reformative, unless it is recognized by the person being punished as JUST, and therefore retributive or deserved.[8]

Once these Christian concepts of responsibility and retribution are discarded from our criminal law and penal system there is absolutely nothing left to hinder our social scientists from using penal measures against persons who, as matters now stand, would be exempt from such "scientific" manipulation upon grounds of mental disorder. Thus it could be argued, as indeed it was argued in Nazi Germany that it is, if anything, more reasonable to execute an insane rather than a sane person since the latter might be more likely to respond favourably to some alternative treatment. Once you throw out the Christian doctrine of responsibility and retribution for wrong doing and replace it with the concept of "treatment," there is absolutely nothing left to hinder the Governments of America and Britain from imprisoning any citizen it dislikes for his political opinions, e.g. Major-General Walker. The principal danger in fact of the proposed "social engineering" and of its subdivisions such as "mental health" is that it equates the political and legal philosophy of apostate humanistic social science with sanity and "right thinking" and brands all opposition as sickness. In his book THE GREAT ENTERPRISE, Dr. H. A. Overstreet writes:—

"A man, for example, may be angrily against racial equality, public housing, the Tennessee Valley Authority, financial and technical aid to backward countries, organized labour and the preaching of social rather than salvational religion . . . Such people may appear 'normal' in the sense that they are able to hold down a job and otherwise maintain their status as members of society, but they are, WE NOW RECOGNIZE, WELL ALONG THE ROAD TOWARD MENTAL ILLNESS."[9]

In terms of such a definition, a person cannot be considered to be healthy and well adjusted unless he or she has first discarded all Christian moral standards, believes in a socialistically "planned economy" and a totalitarian world government.

Now we are being asked in the name of medicine rather than of morals to replace the McNaghten Rules with a new concept that will define ALL criminals as sick if not insane. Let every American beware! Once we eliminate these clear definitions of insanity as laid down in the McNaghten formula and replace it with these new ideas based upon medicine, we shall be on the slippery slope which leads to the elimination of the whole idea of criminal responsibility and its replacement by a question of treatment.

According to the penological system which we are

asked to adopt, medical crimes are those that doctors treat and the crimes that doctors treat are medical crimes. It would seem that the medical world is not afraid of such tautologies. They are for example of a piece with the astonishing definition of mental illness recommended for statutory use by the Committee on Psychiatry and Law of the (U. S.) Group for the Advancement of Psychiatry. According to this definition:—

" 'Mental illness' shall mean an illness which so lessens the capacity of a person to use (maintain) his judgment, discretion and control in the conduct of his affairs and social relations as to warrant his commitment to a mental institution."[10]

By this formula, be it noted, committal to an institution is justified by the presence of mental illness, yet this illness is itself defined only in terms of the need for committal. Under this definition wrongful detention in a mental institution becomes impossible, inasmuch as no room is left for any criterion of health and sickness other than the fact of committal. Far from being disturbed by this gross invasion of the liberties of the subject, however, the same Committee which drafted it would go even further and would revise the American criminal codes in such a way that no person could be "convicted of any criminal charge when at the time he committed the act with which he is charged he was suffering with mental illness" as thus defined, "and in consequence thereof, he committed the act." Those who determine fitness for committal by a criterion which makes their judgment infallible would thus consequentially determine with supposed equal infallibility the question of moral responsibility. No Communist dictator could ask for more. For example suppose an individual became obnoxious to the government in power. Upon being accused of a felony he could be held at Her Majesty's or the President's good pleasure for an indeterminate period in a mental institution on the grounds that he was mentally sick. Already law reformers in Canada are advocating the right for the Government to treat alcoholics and drug addicts not as persons guilty of any objective crime but as sick persons in need of treatment. Thus the Medico-Legal Society of Toronto in a report recently demanded that:—

"Effective treatment of alcoholism requires early COMPULSORY, immediate and continuous long term control of the patient."[11]

In a proposed new Habitue Act the same society would incorporate such a gross infringement of the liberties of the subject by demanding "the immediate apprehension and early treatment of a compulsory nature for an habitue." By adroitly identifying sickness with sin these social scientists would deprive us of our right to be sinful or in their terms sick.

Nowhere, indeed, is this new so-called "scientific" approach to crime more full of logical absurdities than in the proposed treatment of psychopaths. By definition we are told that the psychopath should now be classified as sick rather than sinful.

If present trends continue the category of psychopath will prove to be the Trojan horse that ultimately will shatter the fundamental principles upon which our whole legal and political system is based—undermining the principle of the responsibility of every sane adult for his own actions, his freedom to choose between good and evil, and his liability to be punished should he prefer evil.

Once we have surrendered all OBJECTIVE standards of morality and of individual responsibility we shall place ourselves at the mercy of so called "expert" social scientists. Merciful though their methods of "treatment" may appear at first sight, their adoption in effect would mean that every citizen from the moment he or she breaks the law would find himself or herself deprived of the rights of a human being, of a PERSON created in God's image. By removing the concept of retribution and just desert in punishment the penologists have in fact reduced the offender from being a moral subject to an object for scientific manipulation on the part of psychiatrists. It is only as deserved or underserved that a sentence can be just or unjust. After the new "scientific" method of treating criminals has replaced our present Christian system of punishing them, it will be useless for the rest of us to object that such scientific treatment is "unjust" since the experts will with perfect logic on their side reply, "But nobody is now talking about just deserts. No one is talking of punishment in your archaic vindictive sense of the word. We no longer think of Convict X as a person but as a psychological function of his heredity and environment." The scientistic theory of the cause and cure of crime inevitably has this effect because scientific doctrine is forced by its own methods to REDUCE man to one of his aspects, in this case his psychological and biological aspect. What such treatment amounts to is that the psychiatrist is treating his criminal patient as a THING by means of psycho-analysis and the use of wonder drugs. Most people would prefer to be punished for definite acts of wrong doing than to be "TREATED" in this impersonal way by so-called medical legal experts. Men and women even though guilty of crime are not rats and guinea pigs.[12]

The medical theory of the cause and cure of crime would remove sentences from the hands of jurists and place them in the hands of technical experts whose special sciences refuse to recognize that the criminal is created in God's image and whose express purpose is to destroy all traditional concepts of morality and justice.

Our social scientists are bent on cutting down the authority of our Courts of Law in determining punishment not only in murder cases but in all crimes of a pathological nature. The function of our Courts would be limited to determining the accused person's state of mental health. If he is found to be "unhealthy" he would go for an indefinite term to a mental health centre, only to be released upon the recommendation of some Parole Board. It is admitted by many penologists that this might involve a longer period of preventive detention than the law now imposes for particular offenses.

Such a procedure would be a thoroughly retrogressive step disregarding all our basic civil liberties. It required centuries of struggle to establish the principle that Government officials and experts had no right to hold men in prison indefinitely at their will and pleasure. A great civil war was actually fought out in England partly over the injustices caused by the Court of Star Chamber and to establish the great principle that prison sentences can only be imposed by the Courts AFTER due process of trial and conviction before a jury of one's peers and according to KNOWN and objective rules of law. Modern penologists would now have us scrap this safeguard of our Christian liberties and return to one group of officials—the members of the various Parole Boards and their medical advisers—the same right of arbitrary arrest and indefinite imprisonment which our Puritan ancestors refused to allow the Stuart Kings.

Our tradition that a Court is the proper authority to impose punishment is based on sound reasons. The trial judge is presumably impartial. He has heard all the evidence and he has examined the accused's record. The prisoner has an opportunity to be heard on his own behalf and to be defended by trained lawyers. ABOVE ALL THE PROCEEDINGS ARE OPEN SO THAT THE PUBLIC WILL KNOW IF THERE HAS BEEN A MISCARRIAGE OF JUSTICE. Will these safeguards be present if a prisoner's fate is determined by some secret conclave of psychiatrists and prison wardens under the authority of the National or Federal Parole Board?

What is thus at stake in this whole question is something quite simple. It is fundamentally a question of whether our criminal code is to remain upon OBJECTIVE principles of Justice derived from and based upon God's Revealed Moral Law or whether our criminal code and penal administration is to become SUBJECTIVE, depending upon the shifting sands of psychological medicine. Most English-speaking persons still prefer to be judged and sentenced in a court of law for what they DID wrong than to be treated by some so-called medical expert for what he thinks they ARE. In short the vast majority of English-speaking people still want their criminal law to reflect the objective principles of God's Absolute Moral Standards than to have it become the function of a so-called scientific theory of the cause and treatment of crime. As Christians we are not prepared to let the psychiatrists and penologists do for our morals and penal laws what Darwin and Thomas Huxley did for our pedigree.

References

1. A. V. Dicey. LAW OF THE CONSTITUTION. 8th ed. Macmillan. p. 207.
2. A. V. Dicey. ibid. p. 208.
3. W. B. Munro. THE CONSTITUTION OF THE UNITED STATES. Macmillan, New York, 1930. p. 57.
4. N. Micklem. LAW AND THE LAWS, Sweet and Maxwell, London, Eng., p. 18ff.
5. Edward Glover, THE ROOTS OF CRIME. Preface p. ix. Imago Publishing Company, London, 1960.
6. Report of the Council for Social Service of the United Church of Canada, 1961. 299 Queen St. Toronto, Canada.
7. J. M. Spier, AN INTRODUCTION TO CHRISTIAN PHILOSOPHY. Presbyterian and Reformed Publishing Co., Philadelphia, 1954, p. 15.
8. Norman St. John Stevas. Life, Death and the Law, Eyre and Spottiswoode Emil Brunner. Justice and the Social

Order. Lutterworth, London. A.E.C. Ewing. Morality of Punishment.
Frank Pakenham, Lord Longford. The Idea of Punishment. Chapman, London, 1961.

9. H. A. Overstreet, The Great Enterprise, p. 48.

10. Group for the Advancement of Psychiatry, Criminal Responsibility and Psychiatric Expert Testimony. Report No. 26. Committee on Psychiatry and Law. Topeka, Kansas, 1954, p. 8.

11. Report of the Anglican Council for Social Service, 1959, 600 Jarvis Street, Toronto, Canada, p. 31.

12. C. S. Lewis, The Humanitarian Theory of Punishment. 20th Century 12 Sackville St., Kew E. 4, Victoria, Australia, also, C. S. Lewis, THE ABOLITION OF MAN, Bles, London, 1947.

VIII

A Bible Study

by

GERVAS A. CAREY

"THOU SHALT NOT KILL"

Capital punishment is a subject in which there is widespread interest. While many consider that it is one of the essentials of good government others are equally convinced that it is a hang-over from the middle ages. Between these extremes may be found many arguments both for and against the death penalty. These are advanced from such fields of thought as history, criminology, penology, government and religion.

In the field of religion with which this discussion is primarily concerned, the most surprising argument is being advanced by many who consider themselves careful Bible students. This is the statement that the death penalty for murder is a violation of the Sixth Commandment, "Thou shalt not kill" (Exodus 20:13).

In the first place, attention should be called to the fact that the Ten Commandments were a basic part of the Mosiac Law. This was given by God at Mt. Sinai for the government of the twelve tribes of Israel, who under the leadership of Moses were then en route from their captivity in Egypt to the promised land. These laws as then given were directed to no other people or nation in the world.

In the second place, within the Mosaic Law the Ten Commandments were pointed to individuals as any careful reading will show. Other parts of the Law were intended for the nation as a whole, or for various groups within it, but the Ten Commandments were given to establish standards of personal conduct. The Sixth Commandment was no other than a direct warning against murder by any individual. Neither the text nor context warrants any other conclusion.

In the third place, the inconsistency of using this argument against capital punishment appears in the very next chapter, Exodus 21, in which the death penalty was specifically ordered by law for murder, striking or cursing a parent and for kidnaping (Exodus 21:12-17). Also according to verses 28-29 it was the announced penalty for the owner of any ox which killed a man or woman, if that ox had been known to have gored a person previously.

Other crimes punishable by death under the Mosaic Law may be listed as follows:

adultery, Leviticus 20:10 ff; Deuteronomy 22:23-27;

incest, Leviticus 20:11-12, 14;

bestiality, Exodus 22:19; Leviticus 20:15-16;

sodomy, Leviticus 20:13;

unchastity, Deuteronomy 22:20-21;

rape of a betrothed virgin, Deuteronomy 22:23-27;

witchcraft, Exodus 22:18;

offering human sacrifice, Leviticus 20:2-5;

disobedience to parents, Deuteronomy 21:18-21

blasphemy, Leviticus 24:11-14, 16, 23;

sabbath desecration, Exodus 35:2; Numbers 15:32-36;

propagation of false doctrines, Deuteronomy 13:1-10;

sacrificing to false gods, Exodus 22:20;

refusing to abide by court decision, Deuteronomy 17:8-12;

treason, I Kings 2:19-25.

According to the Biblical narratives capital punishment was administered in various ways. Some of these were:

burning, Leviticus 20:14, 21:9;

stoning, Leviticus 20:2, 27, 24:14;

hanging, Deuteronomy 21:22-23; Joshua 8:29;

the sword, Exodus 32:27-28; I Kings 2:25, 34, 46.

Capital punishment was never to be inflicted on the testimony of less than two witnesses (Numbers 35:30; Deuteronomy 17:6, 19:15). In specified instances capital punishment was to be executed by the witnesses themselves as in Deuteronomy 13:6-10, 17:7. In some instances execution was by the congregation (Numbers 15:32-36; Deuteronomy 13:6-10), or by nearest of kin, the avenger of blood (Deuteronomy 19:11-12).

There were some crimes for which expiation could be made by payment of satisfaction, but murder was not one of these. In Numbers 35:31 it is stated: "Moreover ye shall take no satisfaction for the life of a murderer, which is guilty of death; but he shall be surely put to death."

Attention should be called, however, to the divine provision for the distinction between intentional and accidental killing, now distinguished as first or second degree murder or manslaughter. Cities of refuge were assigned to which a killer might flee for a trial and for continued refuge if not guilty of purposeful murder for which alone the death penalty was prescribed (Numbers 35:9-34).

A major part of the Mosiac Law concerned an extensive ritual of sacrificial and priestly services. These were centered around the tabernacle of the wilderness and the temples of Solomon, Zerubbabel and Herod in order in Jerusalem. Throughout the centuries from the days of Moses to the birth of Jesus the observance of the entire Mosiac Law, both civil and religious, varied from time to time according to the current loyalty and faithfulness of the Israelites and their leaders.

The birth, infancy and childhood of Jesus occurred within the framework of the Mosiac Law and ritual. Early in his ministry Jesus undertook to impress upon his hearers the fact that the Law was a means to an end rather than an end in itself. Its objective forms were designed to teach subjective spiritual realities. In this connection early in the Sermon on the Mount Jesus declared according to Matthew 5:17: "Think not that I am come to destroy the law, or the prophets: I am not come to destroy, but to fulfill."

Later in the sermon he reviewed the requirements

of the Law of Moses and reinterpreted their significance in the light of his teaching. Individual violations of the Ten Commandments should no longer be determined by outward actions but by inward desires. Hence the Sermon on the Mount has been referred to as the constitution of the kingdom of our Lord, in reality a spiritual order.

At no point did his sermon refer to human rule of a civil state in which men are judged by their outward actions rather than by their subjective desires. Naturally God alone can judge guilt on the latter basis. In the light of his teaching the Sixth Commandment was reinterpreted to imply, "Thou shalt not hate."

Later Jesus further indicated his judgment relative to the letter of the law of the commandments after he had been asked by a scribe to indicate the first commandment of all. He replied: "And thou shalt love the Lord thy God with all thy heart, and with all thy soul, and with all thy mind, and with all thy strength: this is the first commandment. And the second is like, namely this, Thou shalt love thy neighbor as thyself" (Mark 12:30-31).

By this statement Jesus further modified the commandments. He removed them from the realm of negations to include them in that of the positives, "Thou shalt love thy neighbor as thyself." Paul later repeated this statement of the essence of the law for the individual. In Galatians 5:14 he declared, "For all the law is fulfilled in one word, even in this; Thou shalt love thy neighbor as thyself."

Jesus fulfilled the Law of Moses by his life and by his death. He conformed to its civil and religious requirements as no other man had ever been able to do. Thereby "Christ hath redeemed us from the curse of the law, being made a curse for us: for it is written, Cursed is everyone that hangeth on a tree" (Galatians 3:13).

The divine purpose of the Mosaic Law is indicated in Galatians 3:24: "Wherefore the law was our schoolmaster to bring us unto Christ, that we might be justified by faith." It follows that we are not living under the law but under grace.

In the light of the preceding discussion it must appear clearly that the Sixth Commandment, "Thou shalt not kill," cannot properly be used as an argument against capital punishment in present day civil government. It was first of all local in its ruling to Israel alone. Furthermore it was a directive against murder on the part of an individual for which capital punishment was the prescribed penalty.

It remained such until Jesus lifted it from the plane of action and placed it within the bounds of attitudes and desires. His emphasis was upon the fact that hatred was the basic sin to be avoided. He later gave it a positive aspect in his inclusive summary, "Thou shalt love thy neighbor as thyself." In all of these relationships it continued in its application to individuals alone. From the days of Moses to Jesus it was never addressed to any governmental body.

GENESIS 9:5-6

It is stated in Genesis 1:31a that upon the completion of creation, "God saw everything that he had made, and, behold it was very good." But some centuries later according to 6:5-8:

"God saw that the wickedness of man was great in the earth, and that every imagination of the thoughts of his heart was only evil continually.

"And it repented the LORD that he had made man on the earth, and it grieved him at his heart.

"And the LORD said, I will destroy man whom I have created from the face of the earth; both man, and beast, and the creeping thing, and the fowls of the air; for it repenteth me that I have made them.

"But Noah found grace in the eyes of the LORD."

When one reads the Bible in order from the beginning there are but five chapters preceding the account of the flood. This account occupies the major part of three chapters.

In the latter part of chapter eight Noah came forth from the ark after the flood and built an altar unto the LORD. Upon this altar he offered burnt offerings of the clean beasts and fowl which had been saved in the ark.

The LORD responded with a pledge to Himself that He would not again curse the ground for man's sake or smite every living thing as He had done. He further promised the continuation of seedtime and harvest with the rotation of the seasons. God blessed Noah and his sons, with the added instruction, "Be fruitful, and multiply, and replenish the earth." The fear and dread of man was placed upon all living creatures while the flesh of animals was assigned to man for food in addition to green herbs.

Thereafter God continued his instructions as recorded in the King James Version in Genesis 9:

"4 But flesh with the life thereof, which is the blood thereof, shall ye not eat.

"5 And surely your blood of your lives will I require; at the hand of every beast will I require it, and at the hand of man; at the hand of every man's brother will I require the life of man.

"6 Whoso sheddeth man's blood, by man shall his blood be shed; for in the image of God made he man.

"7 And you, be ye fruitful, and multiply; bring forth abundantly in the earth, and multiply therein."

The record continues in verses 8-16 with the divine establishment of a covenant with man and with every living creature of the earth that there will never be another flood to destroy the earth. The rainbow was then designated as a seal or token of that covenant.

These promises and instructions were given to Noah, the head of the human race at that time, relative to the establishment of a new social order and government in the world following the flood. It thus appears that the divine decree of capital punishment for murder has been determined since the days of Noah. It should be noted that the basis of this decree as stated in the final clause of verse 6 is as enduring as God and the image of God in which man had been created.

Now in the last half of the twentieth century A.D. it is recognized that the seasons have continued in their order since the time of Noah, with seedtime and harvest, together with cold and heat, summer and winter, and day and night in accordance with the divine promise. Wild animals are still known to exhibit as a rule the fear and dread of man. The flesh of animals is used for food by men throughout the larger part of the world. There has never been another world-destroying flood, while the rainbow continues to be cited as the divine seal of the pledge that never again will there be such.

It therefore appears reasonable to insist that the decree of Genesis 9:5-6 is equally enduring and cannot be separated from the other pledges and instructions of its immediate context, Genesis 8:20-9:17. Certainly that is true unless specific Biblical authority can be cited for the deletion, of which there appears to be none.

Hunts to the death for man-killing animals have been common throughout history. The laws of various early nations during the centuries following the time of Noah down to the present have embodied the penalty of capital punishment for murder. This fact may be coupled with the quite common existence among these nations of a tradition of an early flood. Both of these circumstances afford evidence of the unity of the race with its common descent from Noah. It is true that in some of the European nations and American states the penalty of capital punishment has been repealed. But in some of these it has been re-enacted.

It seems strange that any opponents of capital punishment who profess to recognize the authority of the Bible either overlook or disregard the divine decree in this covenant with Noah and his sons as heads of the human race following the flood. It is both positive and plain in its statement with a logical reason given for its pronouncement.

Thus simply and briefly is presented the Biblical basis of capital punishment. Its institution was imbedded in a context of divine promises which are generally recognized by Bible students as still being in force. No satisfactory Biblical evidence has been produced to justify the removal of Genesis 9:5-6 from the text itself or to explain its being of any less authority than the other portions of Genesis 8:20-9:17. Until such has been produced capital punishment should be recognized by Bible students as the divinely instituted penalty for murder.

ETERNAL LIFE

Within the Bible itself, so far as the writer has been able to discover, the early decree of Genesis 9:6, "Whoso sheddeth man's blood, by man shall his blood be shed," was never repealed. It should be kept in mind that this regulation antedated the Mosaic Law many centuries and appears in Genesis as a part of an entirely independent dealing of God with Noah, the new head of the human race. The basis of this decree, as stated earlier, is as enduring as God and the image of God in which man was created. The reason as assigned by God Himself is specifically stated in the later part of the verse, "for in the image of God made he man."

In the light of this final statement murder not only deprives a man of a portion of his earthly life. It is a further sin against him as a creature made in the image of God and against God Himself whose image the murderer does not respect.

Not only is there no later reference in the Bible to indicate the repeal of Genesis 9:6 but in the New Testament it appears that Jesus declared a principle in practical agreement with it. At the close of His ministry, the night of His arrest in the Garden of Gethsemane, Peter drew his sword and smote the servant of the High Priest, cutting off his ear. For this act Jesus rebuked Peter with the words: "Put up again thy sword into his place: for all they that take the sword shall perish with the sword" (Matthew 26:52).

People quite generally have interpreted this statement to apply to international relations, assuming that it applied to the ultimate effect of militarism within a nation. But these words, however, were addressed to an individual as a rebuke for his personal attack with a deadly weapon and injury to another individual. The statement may possibly be likewise applicable to a nation, but certainly the context requires that the personal reference be given first consideration.

There is also one other pertinent reference in the New Testament. In Galatians 6:7 Paul wrote: "Be not deceived; God is not mocked: for whatsoever a man soweth, that shall he also reap." Murder cannot reasonably be excluded from this all inclusive "whatsoever."

The executioner is not designated in any of these references beyond the usage of the term "man" in Genesis 9:6. But as applied to individual citizens or nations in organized society it must be some individual or agency endowed with civil authority. Each of the three statements cited implies retributive action under divine sanction. And furthermore each of the three statements is primarily concerned with individual action rather than national, if indeed the latter was also divinely intended.

"Certainly," someone will suggest, "the love of God cannot be discovered in capital punishment." Any proper appreciation of the facts here involved depends on a right understanding of life, here and hereafter, as taught in the Bible. Man's physical life is not, as many people believe, his most valuable possession. It is secondary in that at its longest, which at present may be even eighty to a hundred years, it is but an incident compared with eternal existence. A man's opportunity to prepare for eternal life in reality is his most valuable possession.

During World War II an acquaintance, a minister in a nearby village, had a son of draft age. He had been deferred from service call until after his high school graduation. He then took his basic training, after which he came home on his final furlough before going overseas.

Naturally his father and mother were concerned as to his safety in the service in Europe where he was being sent. He had been a fine Christian young man and finally said to his father, "But Dad, if we really believe in eternal life, what difference does it make as to how much of it we spend here?"

He was sent overseas where he was killed in the early days of the Normandy invasion. His father stated to the writer afterward that the son's faith and above all his sane Christian evaluation of life here and hereafter had been a source of great comfort to them in their sorrow.

Surely that father could be far more thankful to God in review of his son's brief life than to have known later that he had lived many years longer and died in sin. The son now has no reason to regret the brevity of his earthly life.

Following the foregoing digression a return will be made to a more direct consideration of capital punishment. In Ecclesiastes 8:11 it is stated: "Because sentence against an evil work is not executed speedily, therefore the heart of the sons of men is fully set in them to do evil." This declaration suggests that the remoteness of punishment may leave even murderers unrestrained.

A murderer sentenced to life imprisonment naturally is seldom interested in his soul's welfare. He is more inclined to plan his escape or to dwell in thought upon the time and means which he hopes will bring him a parole. The modern criminal treatment provides but slight evidence on the basis of which any lifer needs to question the possibility of his ultimate release from prison.

A sentence of capital punishment pronounced with assurance of its execution places a murderer in an entirely different situation. A date for his execution is set. Procrastination need no longer be the thief of time. Yet even in the death cell the murderer may or may not repent. However, it may be stated with assurance that if he has expected to do so some day, he can see the limit of this possibility.

It may not be amiss to suggest that therein a secondary measure of the love of God may be said to appear. For capital punishment provides the murderer with an incentive to repentance which the ordinary man does not have, that is a definite date on which he is to meet his God. It is as if God thus providentially granted him a special inducement to repentance out of consideration of the enormity of his crime.

The murderer has dishonored God and man by having taken a human life created in the image of God. Life was as dear to the murdered as is his to the murderer. In most cases the victim had been killed with no opportunity to get right with his Creator if he had not already done so. Capital punishment decrees that the murderer shall give his life, after due trial and legal conviction, as a penalty for his affront to God and retribution for the human life taken. The law grants to the condemned an opportunity which he did not grant to his victim, the opportunity to prepare to meet his God. Even divine justice here may be said to be tempered with mercy.

The subject of capital punishment has long been a controversial one. In early times it was disgracefully used by application to so many minor offenses. The later trends have been to limit it to first degree murder or to that with rape and kidnaping for ransom included. It has been entirely discontinued in several states, in some of which it was later restored.

Those who argue against it usually urge that it does not deter crime. Anyone, however, will be forced to admit that it does deter the executed criminal from further crime. There can be no question in regard to Bruno Hauptmann or the more recently notorious pair of Hall and Heady. They will never again kidnap a wealthy man's son for ransom and then kill him before their demand for ransom is made as was done by the three named.

It is life imprisonment which does not deter crime. All too many lifers have committed other murders in prison or later while out on parole. But it should be noted particularly that the Bible presents capital punishment as a just penalty for a serious crime committed. There is no suggestion in Genesis 9:5-6 that any deterrent effect on others was intended.

Yet God loves murderers sentenced to death and Jesus died to save them if they will repent and accept Him. God alone knows certainly whether they repent sincerely and seek forgiveness prior to their execution. They definitely are not excluded from the divine promise, "whosoever shall call on the name of the Lord shall be saved."

At least during their final days in the death cell they cannot avoid the fact that they are facing the end of their earthly life. At some point it must dawn upon them that it is futile to give further thought to plans for escape. Sentence is now to be executed speedily.

The two robbers who were crucified with Jesus were both sentenced to death for what now appears to have been a minor crime. Yet to the one capital punishment proved to be a great blessing. It brought him face to face with Jesus Christ, his Saviour.

Doubtless among his eternal praises to God there may be at times an expression of gratitude for the cross of crucifixion. Likewise even some murderers may praise God for capital punishment which brought them to themselves and their Saviour.

According to Genesis 9:5-6 divine justice requires that a murderer pay for his crime with his own physical life. But divine love may be said to be standing alongside to announce clearly the words of John 3:36: "He that believeth on the Son hath everlasting life." This is the gift of the love of God, available to anyone who will accept the provisions of God's grace. If, as it did for the thief on the cross, capital punishment brings any murderer face to face with his Saviour in true penitence, the ultimate love of God will triumph on his behalf. On the other hand, if he refuses to accept Christ, he must do so with the definite knowledge that he is rejecting his last opportunity for eternal life. Then the further statement of John 3:36 will be applicable to him: "and he that believeth not the Son shall not see life; but the wrath of God abideth on him."

The thought of capital punishment is not a pleasant one on which to dwell. Neither are the many other judgments of God as described in both the Old and the New Testaments. But God-fearing men should seek to be guided by the word of God rather than by their emotions or personal rationalizations.

It was because of his disobedience that Moses had failed to sanctify God in the midst of the children of Israel at the waters of Meribah (Numbers 20:1-13). On this account he was forbidden to enter the promised land. Instead, God sentenced him to an earlier death on Mt. Nebo, while in robust health, although he was permitted to view the land from the mountain top. This was a sore disappointment to Moses, yet on the eve of his death under these circumstances he wrote:

"Because I will publish the name of the LORD: ascribe ye greatness unto our God.

"He is the Rock, his work is perfect: for all his ways are judgment: a God of truth and without iniquity, just and right is he" (Deuteronomy 32:3-4).

OBJECTIONS
BASED ON THE BIBLE

OBJECTION 1—

God Himself spared Cain and protected him after he had killed Abel, the first murder on record.

ANSWER—

That is true. No explanation as to the reason for this is given in the Bible. However, by the time of Noah the wickedness of man is said to have become so great that "it repented the LORD that he had made man on the earth" (Genesis 6:5-6). This is indicated to have been the reason for the flood. In the absence of any specific statement it appears probable that the LORD likewise repented of his lenient treatment of Cain.

The centuries between Cain and Noah are covered very briefly with lists of Cain's and Seth's descendants. The only mention of murder during this interim is that by the braggart Lamech in Genesis 4:23. Yet it seems natural to believe that murder must have entered more largely than that into the conditions as described in Chapter 6:5. "And God saw that the wickedness of man was great in the earth, and that every imagination of the thoughts of his heart was only evil continually." That this general wickedness of man included widespread murder is further suggested by the statement of Jesus in Matthew 15:19, that murder is one of the issues of the human heart; while Paul lists it as one of the works of the flesh in Galatians 5:21.

The divine treatment of Cain was an individual matter. But Genesis 9:5-6 contains a later general decree for application to all murderers thereafter. Both are attributed to the LORD with centuries intervening. They are unrelated in the Genesis text.

OBJECTION 2—

Genesis 9:5-6 is in the Old Testament which is outdated.

ANSWER—

Jesus cited the Old Testament in John 10:34-36, adding this parenthetical statement, "And the scripture cannot be broken." The Christian church has continued to use the Old Testament throughout the centuries as the basic foundation of its faith in the Christ of the New Testament.

OBJECTION 3—

Moses was not executed for his murder of the Egyptian.

ANSWER—

The Israelites were then slaves in Egypt, hence under the rule of the Pharaohs. It is stated that Moses fled from Egypt in order to save his life.

Otherwise he would have been killed by or at the order of the king.

OBJECTION 4—

David was not executed for his adultery with Bathsheba and murder of her husband, Uriah the Hittite.

ANSWER—

David lived under the Mosaic Law. He committed two crimes, adultery and murder, both of which were punishable by death under that law. This fact apparently was recognized by the prophet Nathan and the king also, in the light of Nathan's statement to David: "The LORD also hath put away thy sins; thou shalt not die" (II Samuel 12:13).

In the Old Testament the prophets were spokesmen for God. No reason is assigned for this special divine dispensation on David's behalf. Nathan was not speaking on his own initiative.

Divine wisdom may have recognized that the agony in the repentance of David as expressed in the 51st Psalm and his later suffering in his own family and kingdom would be an effective lesson for later generations, as they have been. But this is only a human supposition. We cannot certainly fathom the wisdom of God beyond what is written.

OBJECTION 5—

Jesus did away with the Law, hence Genesis 9:5-6 is not now in effect.

ANSWER—

Jesus did away with the Law of Moses by his fulfillment of the same. But there is no evidence in the Bible that the covenant of God with Noah and the

Law of Moses were ever associated in any way. The covenant with Noah was worldwide in its application, while the Law of Moses was directed to the twelve tribes of Israel alone, centuries later than the time of Noah.

OBJECTION 6—

Jesus said, "Ye have heard that it hath been said, An eye for an eye, and a tooth for a tooth: But I say unto you, That ye resist not evil: but whosoever shall smite thee on thy right cheek, turn to him the other also" (Matthew 5:38-39).

ANSWER—

This is very clearly an instruction concerning personal action, not for civil regulation.

OBJECTION 7—

Jesus did not order the woman taken in adultery stoned, but told her to go her way, "and sin no more" (John 8:2-11).

ANSWER—

It should be noted that the scribes and Pharisees had taken this woman to Jesus rather than to a legal magistrate. This was done because they were primarily interested in an attempt to entangle Jesus rather than to secure the conviction of the woman. They certainly were well aware of the fact that the Roman law at that time did not permit the Jews to inflict the death penalty on anyone. Jews generally recognized this according to later statement in Objection 8.

As usual, however, Jesus was equal to any challenge. Concerning His first coming He later stated, "I came not to judge the world, but to save the world" (John 12:47). He did not thereby discredit judgment but stated His earthly mission at the time. Elsewhere He stated that He will act in judgment at His Second Coming (Matthew 13:40-43).

OBJECTION 8—

The Jews told Pilate that it was not lawful for them to put anyone to death (John 18:31).

ANSWER—

They were here referring to the law of Rome with its limitation on their independent action in regard to the death penalty. Hence they were seeking the authorization of the Roman governor for the conviction of Jesus.

OBJECTION 9—

Saul of Tarsus was not executed for his part in the stoning of Stephen.

ANSWER—

The stoning of Stephen in the end appears to have been a mob action, although a hearing was held before the council. But as noted in connection with Objection 8, even the council did not have authority of Rome to pass the death sentence. The use of the term "witnesses" indicated that from the Jewish standpoint they were holding a formal trial which ended in the mob action of stoning. As a loyal Jew Saul's action in participation was not that of a murderer in the eyes of the council or any of its leaders. He was no more guilty than any of the others.

OBJECTION 10—

"God is love." How can a God of love direct the putting of anyone to death?

ANSWER—

This objection either evades or does not recognize the fact that there can be no true love devoid of justice. God is love, but he is not an indulgent Father who can overlook or excuse the sins of his children. There may have been periods in the history of the Christian church when the judgments of God were overemphasized, but the present tendency is to go to the other extreme. *John 3:16 states the measure of the love of God while verses 18 and 36 recognize the unique association of both love and justice, in that they are really inseparable in God.* The wrath of God is reserved for those who refuse His mercy.

OBJECTION 11—

To God alone belongs the right of life and of death. Let God be God.

ANSWER—

The first statement is correct. But how can anyone let God be God while at the same time refusing or denying His will as explicitly stated in regard to the punishment of the murderer?

OBJECTION 12—

Progress in the human understanding of God first gives us a view of the stern vindictive God of the Old Testament which gives way to the tender loving character of Jesus Christ in the New Testament.

ANSWER—

The objection as stated recognizes but a part of the truth in both Testaments. The element of tender love is also to be found in many places in the Old Testament while many references also bear witness to the stern attitude of Jesus Christ in the New

Testament. His attitude was unyielding toward sin and unrepentant sinners. The God of the Old Testament is the God of the New Testament, in actual being variously revealed but never progressively contradictory as suggested.

OBJECTIONS
IN GENERAL

OBJECTION 1—

Capital punishment results in a double standard of justice, hence should be abolished. This statement is usually introduced or supported by a quotation from ex-Warden Lawes of Sing Sing prison to the effect that he had never known of the execution of a wealthy man. He claimed that only the poor, or men of moderate means who had been unable to hire highly skilled criminal lawyers ever face the death penalty. This is a widely used argument by both British and American writers opposed to capital punishment.

ANSWER—

Basically this statement really presents no argument against capital punishment. It is rather a confession of the maladministration of justice. If applied in accordance with its logic it would require the repeal of every penalty on the statute books, as it is doubtful whether there is any country in the world in which all criminal laws have been applied impartially at all times to the rich and poor alike.

Micah, one of the Old Testament prophets who lived several centuries before the time of Christ, has been designated "The Tribune of the People," because in his day he boldly denounced the oppression and discrimination against the poor. Priests, prophets and judges were all accused for their part in this oppression.

In the United States near the close of the nineteenth century there was a widespread social and economic awakening. In this connection there was current a popular saying that if a poor man should steal a hod of coal from a railroad car to keep his children warm he would be sent to jail, but if a rich man should steal the railroad he would be sent to Congress. But no one then proposed to modify the penalties for theft on that account.

OBJECTION 2—

Capital punishment is no deterrent to murder. Statistics are usually quoted to show the relationship of the number of murders in states or countries with and without the death penalty, or before and after its repeal or restoration.

ANSWER—

The designation "capital punishment" involves in itself no suggestion of deterrence. According to Webster, punishment in a legal sense is, "A penalty inflicted by a court of justice on a convicted offender as a just retribution." Such was its intent as first announced by God in Genesis 9:6: "Whoso sheddeth man's blood, by man shall his blood be shed: for in the image of God made he man." No reference to deterrence of others was made then or later.

This is in keeping with the practiced usage of punishment in the home, school or society. Its effective usage as a just desert of the offender may or may not have a secondary result in the deterrence of others from the same wrong doing. When Johnny's father gave him a whipping for flagrant disobedience it was not administered in the presence of Billy in order to deter him from a similar action. It was Johnny's punishment that was intended.

But at least anyone will have to admit that capital punishment is a deterrent from any repetition of the crime by the executed murderer. As stated in an earlier section neither Bruno Hauptmann nor the more recent notorious pair, Hall and Heady, will ever kidnap another wealthy man's son and kill him prior to their demands for ransom.

OBJECTION 3—

The idea of punishment is outdated. Rehabilitation is the modern concept of the goal for the treatment of all criminals, including murderers. This makes the idea of capital punishment unthinkable for today.

ANSWER—

The rehabilitation advocates are usually also opposed to life imprisonment. But there are many others who are equally certain that this passing of the appreciation of punishment is one of the leading causes of the great increase of crime during recent years.

A noted California judge has recently written an article in which he stated why he believes that a switch in time will keep many youngsters out of court. Bishop Sheen has characterized over-indulgent parents as the curse of the twentieth century. The same may be said of the over-indulgent schools, law officials, courts and all other administrators of justice.

Those who have gone all out for the development of self-expression on the part of children in the homes, schools and in society at large, with no punishments or positive directive controls, must share a large part of the responsibility for this current increase in crime. The practical value of punishment has too long a list of personal acknowledgments to be denied.

Some form of the word punish is used eighty-one times in the King James Version of the Bible. The Old and the New Testaments both state that God punishes evil doers in this life and in the next. In Genesis 9:6 He decreed that man should act as His agent in the punishment of the murderer in this life.

OBJECTION 4—

There is always danger that an innocent man may be executed. It is positively known that such error has happened. Such a tragedy is irreparable.

ANSWER—

These statements are all true. But with all of the modern scientific methods of dealing with crime and procedures of court trials this possibility has become very slight. It is probably no greater, if as great, as that the criminal may commit another murder while serving a long prison sentence or later when out on parole. Both of these possibilities have also occurred.

OBJECTION 5—

Capital punishment does not recognize the sacredness of personality.

ANSWER—

As a matter of fact capital punishment was first enacted out of respect for the sacredness of personality. "For in the image of God made He man" was the reason first assigned for the decree, "Whoso sheddeth man's blood, by man shall his blood be shed". The man who disregards the sacredness of human personality to the extent that he commits murder is the offender. He thereby forfeits any rights to claim the protection of the sacredness of his own life.

OBJECTION 6—

Life imprisonment is a greater punishment than death. Society is amply protected by a sentence of life imprisonment.

ANSWER—

The first sentence might be true if life imprisonment really meant what it says. However, life imprisonment is no longer considered to mean imprisonment for life but for some indefinite period until a parole or pardon may be secured, as is now very generally anticipated. Within a few years the memory of the murdered and all relatives and dependents becomes blurred while a popular sentiment builds up into a demand for the release of the convicted man. With his release society loses whatever measure of absolute protection it had been granted by his imprisonment.

Furthermore, if life imprisonment is a greater punishment than death, its imposition would be exceeding the divine decree of capital punishment for murder. It would be a substitution of cruelty for justice by the order of the court.

OBJECTION 7—

No murderers are normal, hence each should be dealt with in the light of his individual physical and mental condition. Criminals are all sick. They need treatment rather than punishment. Let the punishment fit the criminal rather than the crime.

ANSWER—

There are numerous cases in which the courts determine that men are not sufficiently normal to recognize the distinction between right and wrong. In such cases the criminals are usually committed to mental institutions. But to claim that all murderers are irresponsible, or even partially so, is to undermine all morality. It leads to the conclusion that the same may be said of every lawbreaker. This disregards the fact that men generally have made themselves today the total of their yesterdays. The lack of discipline and self-control in the home and schools and in later life sets the stage for all kinds of crime.

Many thoughtful and observant persons have witnessed with sorrow the transition from innocent childhood to the criminal status, at times slowly or at other times rapidly, with no evidences of physical or mental deficiencies. In fact victims may have been superior in both realms.

OBJECTION 8—

Reluctance to sentence a murderer to capital punishment deters many juries from reaching a just verdict and favors the escape of criminals. Without capital punishment more convictions would be possible with fewer delays.

ANSWER—

In trials for murder where capital punishment is the penalty for first degree, prospective jurors are excused in such instances when opposed to the death penalty. It is equally possible that more and quicker convictions might be secured for many other crimes if the penalties therefor were sufficiently reduced. But justice rather than a speedy conviction should be the end sought in all trials.

OBJECTION 9—

Trial for murder is highly and sensationally publicized in cases where capital punishment may be the penalty. This results in great injury to society in general.

ANSWER—

It is questionable whether sensationalism in this connection is intensified by the fact that capital punishment is the issue. The sensationalism in court and press reports is usually related to the characters involved and the sordidness of the details of the crime. The incidents related and evidences being produced are usually the cause of the sensationalism rather than any question as to the ultimate outcome of the trial and conviction.

OBJECTION 10—

Sentiment against capital punishment is on the rise.

ANSWER—

This may presently be true. But public sentiment as popularly expressed cannot be accepted as a criterion of justice. It is too easily swayed by emotional elements involved in current circumstances.

Many elections have been won or lost by sudden shifts in public sentiment. Capital punishment has been restored where it had earlier been repealed, since an unusually brutal murder arouses public sentiment again in its favor even where it had been abolished.

ADDENDUM

The writer has been asked why he, a minister of the Gospel, should feel called upon to advocate capital punishment. In early manhood the call to preach came to him with a very definite conviction that the Bible is the written word of God, in its entirety, both the Old and the New Testaments. It was in the light of this understanding that he began the habit of reading the Bible through consecutively with the idea that the separate books were really chapters in one book rather than sixty-six books in one library. This habit has been closely adhered to for over fifty years and has resulted in some deep convictions.

The God of the Old Testament is the God of the New Testament. This applies to personality, character and eternal activity. God is love. But there can be no true love apart from justice. In the two Testaments, at different times and places, one aspect of the character of God may stand out more distinctly than elsewhere, but never to the denial of other aspects.

An early recollection of theological discussions is that of repeated charges that in certain periods of the church too much emphasis had been placed upon the judgments of God as applied to sinners. The inference drawn was that the appeal of John 3:16 had been neglected. But in time, following many readings, the idea of judgment in John 3:16 became as vivid as its promise of life. "For God so loved the world, that he gave his only begotten Son, that whosoever believeth in him should not perish; but have everlasting life." The thought of perishing aside from belief is as definite as the promise of life to those who believe. In verse 18 this idea is carried still further in the statement: "but he that believeth not is condemned already, because he has not believed in the name of the only begotten Son of God."

Continued consecutive reading of the entire Bible has brought into clear focus these two ideas; men are perishing in their unbelief, but may be saved through faith in the Son of God, and secondly, men for whom Christ died may reject his love, but surely will be cast into outer darkness for their unrepented sinfulness.

God is love. The disposition of God is to exercise mercy and forgiveness wherever the attitude of man meets the divine requirements. Divine justice demands that the penalty for sin must be met by the sinner himself or by his acceptance of the Son of God as his Substitute and Saviour.

Thus divine justice and divine forgiveness become two dominant ideas of the entire Bible while John 3:16 continues to proclaim this central theme. Men may perish or have eternal life by choice.

If in the pulpits of America there ever was a time when the judgments of God were overemphasized it is very evident that the pendulum has now swung to the opposite extreme. The mercy of God is everlasting. But if it be emphasized to the entire neglect of his judgments there is but a partial compliance with the injunction, "Preach the word" (II Timothy 4:2a).

Naturally those portions of the Bible which deal with the blessings of God and his many promises to believers make a far greater appeal to the average reader than do the accounts of his judgments. Even the most consecrated ministers under the daily pressure of their many duties may find themselves reading brief selected devotional portions of their Bibles to the entire neglect of others. By this course their congregations may be gaining slowly but surely a one-sided appreciation of God as well as of the Bible.

Thus a "soft-line" in the Gospel ministry may gradually take over as it seems to have been doing in the American social, moral and judicial life. The surest safeguard against such would be for all ministers and Christians in general to read their entire Bibles consecutively in addition to other devotional readings of favorite passages.

The acceptance of the Biblical teaching concerning divine judgment should remove some of the principal objections to capital punishment. As noted earlier this appears in Genesis as the divinely appointed punishment for man's greatest social crime. Murder is the result of a disregard of both man and God, in whose image man was created, and calls for the supreme sacrifice of the murderer's life at the hand of man.

Viewed in itself alone this decree of God might seem unreal. But when placed alongside the numerous other judgments of God as recorded in both the Old and New Testaments, it fits into the pattern of divine judgment interwoven with mercy throughout the entire Bible.

It is not necessary to list or even discuss the judgments of God as recorded in the Old Testament. These are many and well known to most Bible readers. But for those who look upon them as merely primitive barbaric customs perpetrated by the Israelites in the name of their God, it may be well to call attention to the continuation of divine judgments throughout the New Testament. These listed quotations are but a few of the many there recorded.

"But whosoever shall say, Thou fool, shall be in danger of hell fire" (Jesus, in Matthew 5:22b).

"But if ye forgive not men their trespasses, neither will your Father forgive your trespasses" (Jesus, in Matthew 6:15).

"The Son of man shall send forth his angels, and they shall gather out of his kingdom all things that offend, and them which do iniquity; And shall cast them into a furnace of fire: there shall be wailing and gnashing of teeth" (Jesus, in Matthew 13:41-42).

"Ye serpents, ye generation of vipers, how can ye escape the damnation of hell?" (Jesus, in Matthew 23:33).

"Then shall he say also unto them on the left hand, Depart from me, ye cursed, into everlasting fire, prepared for the devil and his angels" (Jesus, in Matthew 25:41).

"But he that shall blaspheme against the Holy

Ghost hath never forgiveness, but is in danger of eternal damnation" (Jesus, in Mark 3:29).

"There shall be weeping and gnashing of teeth, when ye shall see Abraham, and Isaac, and Jacob, and all the prophets, in the kingdom of God, and you yourselves thrust out" (Jesus, in Luke 13:28).

"Marvel not at this: for the hour is coming, in the which all that are in the graves shall hear his voice, And shall come forth; they that have done good, unto the resurrection of life; and they that have done evil unto the resurrection of damnation" (Jesus, in John 5:28-29).

"If a man abide not in me, he is cast forth as a branch, and is withered; and men gather them and cast them into the fire, and they are burned" (Jesus, in John 15:6).

"Then Peter said unto her, How is it that ye have agreed together to tempt the Spirit of the Lord? behold, the feet of them which have buried thy husband are at the door, and shall carry thee out. Then fell she down straightway at his feet, and yielded up the ghost" (Acts 5:9-10a).

"And immediately the angel of the Lord smote him, because he gave not God the glory: and he was eaten of worms, and gave up the ghost" (Acts 12:23).

"For the wrath of God is revealed from heaven against all ungodliness and unrighteousness of men, who hold the truth in unrighteousness" (Romans 1:18).

"But unto them that are contentious, and do not obey the truth, but obey unrighteousness, indignation and wrath, Tribulation and anguish, upon every soul of man that doeth evil, of the Jew first, and also of the Gentile" (Romans 2:8-9).

"If any man defile the temple of God, him shall God destroy; for the temple of God is holy, which temple ye are" (I Corinthians 3:17).

"Know ye not that the unrighteous shall not inherit the kingdom of God?" (I Corinthians 6:9a).

"For we must all appear before the judgment seat of Christ; that every one may receive the things done in his body, according to that he hath done, whether it be good or bad" (II Corinthians 5:10).

"Be not deceived; God is not mocked: for whatsoever a man soweth, that shall he also reap" (Galatians 6:7).

"For this ye know, that no whoremonger, nor unclean person, nor covetous man, who is an idolater, hath any inheritance in the kingdom of Christ and of God. Let no man deceive you with vain words: for because of these things cometh the wrath of God upon the children of disobedience" (Ephesians 5:5-6).

"But he that doeth wrong shall receive for the wrong which he hath done: and there is no respect of persons" (Colossians 3:25).

"When the Lord Jesus shall be revealed from heaven with his mighty angels, in flaming fire taking vengeance on them that know not God, and that obey not the gospel of our Lord Jesus Christ: Who shall be punished with everlasting destruction from the presence of the Lord" (II Thessalonians 1:7b-9a).

"If we suffer we shall also reign with him: if we deny him, he also will deny us" (II Timothy 2:12).

"He that despised Moses' law died without mercy under two or three witnesses: Of how much sorer punishment, suppose ye, shall he be thought worthy, who hath trodden under foot the Son of God, and hath counted the blood of the covenant, wherewith he was sanctified, an unholy thing, and hath done despite unto the Spirit of grace?" (Hebrews 10:28-29).

"For the eyes of the Lord are over the righteous, . . . but the face of the Lord is against them that do evil (I Peter 3:12).

"The Lord knoweth how to deliver the godly out of temptations, and to reserve the unjust unto the day of judgment to be punished" (II Peter 2:9).

"But the fearful, and unbelieving, and the abominable, and murderers, and whoremongers, and sorcerers, and idolaters, and all liars, shall have their part in the lake which burneth with fire and brimstone: which is the second death" (Revelation 21:8).

Thus in the inspired word of God divine judgments appear as the continuing backdrop for redemption. *Mercy would seem to be a meaningless term in the Bible otherwise.*

Capital punishment as decreed by God to Noah appears early in this line of judgments. It is consistent therewith and is clearly an integral part of the revealed scriptures. Hence the advocacy of it is no more than complete submission to the will of God. But in fact this is not the personal advocacy of capital punishment. It is rather the proclamation of the divinely directed penalty for murder. It may well be prefaced, or concluded, "Thus saith the LORD God".